BLAKE *and* FREUD

BLAKE *and* FREUD

Diana Hume George

CORNELL UNIVERSITY PRESS

ITHACA AND LONDON

First published 1980 by Cornell University Press.
Published in the United Kingdom by Cornell University Press Ltd.,
2-4 Brook Street, London WIY 1AA.

Excerpts from *The Collected Papers of Sigmund Freud*, edited by Ernest Jones, M.D., in five volumes, are reprinted by permission of Basic Books, Inc., which publishes them in the United States by arrangement with The Hogarth Press, Ltd., and The Institute of Psycho-Analysis, London.

International Standard Book Number 0-8014-1286-2
Library of Congress Catalog Card Number 80-11244
Printed in the United States of America
*Librarians: Library of Congress cataloging information appears
on the last page of the book.*

To Mac Nelson

Contents

Illustrations

Acknowledgments

This book was completed with the assistance of a grant from the American Association of University Women (Gladys Murphy Graham Fellowship, 1977–78). I also gratefully acknowledge the assistance of Murray Schwartz, Diane Christian, and Leslie Fiedler, all of the State University of New York at Buffalo, and Alicia Ostriker of Rutgers University who commented extensively on earlier drafts of *Blake and Freud*. I appreciate the support of other colleagues and friends: Mallory Clifford, Cheryl Bell, and especially Karen Campbell. Of those who share my home and my life, Bernie George, Jr., and Malcolm Nelson, I ask forgiveness. At Cornell University Press I would like to thank Bernhard Kendler, whose interest persuaded me to shape a manuscript of unwieldy length into a study of manageable proportions; Barbara Salazar, whose sure editorial hand transformed barbarisms with remarkable tact, and with an unfailing sense of what I wanted to say when I hadn't said it; and Marilyn Sale, who first suggested Cornell's interest in *Blake and Freud*. Finally, I suspect I owe more thanks to my typist and unofficial critic, Theresa Dispenza, than to all the others combined.

I gratefully acknowledge permission to quote as follows: *The Collected Papers of Sigmund Freud*, edited by Ernest Jones, M.D., in five volumes, published by Basic Books, Inc., by arrangement with The Hogarth Press, Ltd., and The Institute of Psycho-Analysis, London (essays in *The Collected Papers* are also available in *The Standard Edition of the Complete Psychological Works of Sig-*

mund Freud, translated and edited by James Strachey); *Civiliza-tion and Its Discontents*, translated and edited by James Strachey, published by W. W. Norton in the United States, and in Volume 21 of the *Standard Edition*, Sigmund Freud Copyrights Ltd., The Institute of Psycho-Analysis, and The Hogarth Press, Ltd. Unless otherwise noted, all quotations in this volume from the works of William Blake are from *The Poetry and Prose of William Blake*, edited by David V. Erdman, with commentary by Harold Bloom (Garden City, N.Y.: Doubleday, 1970).

D. H. G.

Brocton, New York

BLAKE *and* FREUD

Introduction

"But why aren't you working on Blake and Jung?" When I began this book on Blake and Freud, I was repeatedly asked that question. There seemed no reasonably brief way to counter my colleagues' convictions that if I were explicating Blake as psychologist, I should clearly emphasize archetypes, the collective unconscious, and anima/animus configurations. The single adjective still most frequently applied to Blake is "mystical." It is the connotations of that word, applied to both Blake and Jung, that probably directs the conclusion that they are obvious and congenial bedfellows. A great deal of profitable study indeed remains to be done on Blake and Jung, following June Singer's 1970 study, *The Unholy Bible: A Psychological Interpretation of William Blake*. But the assumption that among psychoanalytic theorists Jung is most "Blakean" and that among poets Blake is most "Jungian" suggests some limiting preconceptions about both Blake and Freud. Behind the question "Why not Blake and Jung?" is an unvoiced assumption that Blake and Freud are utterly antithetical.

In several respects, perhaps they are antithetical. Freud's is the ultimate analytic mind, and the discipline he founded keeps the word "analysis" unaltered in its name. Classification, division, minute examination: these are accurate terms to characterize psychoanalytic method. The language of structuralist and poststructuralist critical theory—such words as "dissemination" and "deconstruction"—reflects an openly acknowledged debt to

Freud, as do the nature and aims of the entire structuralist venture, however one defines that venture. Blake, to continue a schematic simplification of the contrast, is romantic, passionate, unitive, primarily concerned with synthesis rather than analysis, poetry rather than science. Freud is an empiricist, while Blake is vehemently antiempirical. Freud claimed for psychoanalysis the status of a natural science; Blake despised the "Goddess Nature." Blake eventually claimed to dislike classical culture and art, but Freud's collection of Roman artifacts was his dearest possession, and he traced his own scientific roots to Empedocles. Finally, and perhaps most inclusively, Blake declared himself a prophetic visionary, and drew an artificially precise dividing line between visionary and mimetic modes of thinking, writing, being. If we may judge from Blake's estimation of Milton's errors, we cannot doubt that Blake would have placed Sigmund Freud in the same category as Bacon, Newton, and Locke, the villainous presences of Blake's major prophecies. The lack of fellow feeling might have been conveniently mutual. Freud would have had little use for Blake, except perhaps as a fascinating study in neurosis; maybe even pathology.

The Freudian reader is by now weary of such reductive oversimplifications of Freud as the one I have presented. Restricting Freud to the analytic model of mind is rather like saying that because Bach is so highly disciplined, he is also dry, sterile, and passionless. Such simplifications also mistake the nature and scope of deep analysis. The Blakean reader will be equally tired of the litany of half-truths I have chanted about Blake. Blake achieved his synthesis only through penetrating analysis. He did not hate nature; he was countering a historical pattern in the symbolic and psychic imaging of nature. His dislike for classical culture was at least as rhetorical as it was actual.

When the half-truths about Blake and Freud are countered and qualified, the two minds cross an expanse of time and space and meet in what I consider a radical union of poetry and science, synthesis and analysis, romanticism and determinism. They meet through metaphorical process, through the poet in

Freud and the psychoanalyst in Blake. I do not intend these statements as fuzzy, poetic generalities. References to Freud are certainly not new in Blake scholarship, though they are often fuzzy and general or spuriously specific. Works as old as Foster Damon's *Blake Dictionary* make casual references to such terms as id, ego, and superego. Critical studies of Blake are often spiced with oedipal this and phallic that. Freudian terminology sometimes answers the need for a shorthand translation of Blake's mythopoesis into diction better understood by a post-Freudian generation. But the application of what Blake would call "Minute Particulars" is of only limited use without explication of the pattern those particulars form. I find the pattern more Freudian than Jungian, despite the profound similarities between Blake and Jung and the real differences between Blake and Freud.

This book has several major purposes. First, it unabashedly continues a long-standing trend in Blake scholarship, one that is the source of (sometimes legitimate) amusement and contempt outside of the admittedly cultish circle of Blake aficionados. Blakers think Blake knew everything about everything. If we get the chance, we will claim that Blake invented the breadbox, right after he invented bread. I make a large claim for Blake: not only that his work anticipated Freud's, but that his mapping of psychic processes actually subsumes Freud's in several identifiable respects. I do not claim that Blake and Freud agree on every tenet; on the contrary, the points at which Blake's system differs from Freud's are often located precisely where contemporary psychoanalytic theory has found Freud in need of expansion or revision. Specifically, I refer to Freud's theories on sublimation, oedipal configurations, and feminine psychology as foci for revisionism, and to his writings on so-called metapsychology, especially the late works that include implications for the sociocultural application of psychoanalytic theory, as foci for both expansion and revision. Blake's system often points in directions taken by revisionists only after Freud's death, and just as frequently gets where psychoanalysis has yet to go. I intend this study, then, as a contribution to psychoanalytic theory and criticism, regardless of any interest the analytic reader may or may not have in Blake as poet. I regard this book as an introductory study of Blake and Freud because I concentrate primarily on Blake's early works, with extensive but not exhaustive forays into the later prophecies. Similarly, it is also only an introduction to Blake and psychoanalysis, as distinct from Blake and Freud, because the parallels between Blake and psychoanalytic revisionism deserve separate and careful consideration. I can best suggest the tenor of such parallels by locating my work in the context of three major revisionists.

My "revision" of Freud through Blake shares common concerns with the works of Wilhelm Reich, Herbert Marcuse, and Norman O. Brown, though my focus is narrower, less "social," and less specifically derived from an American urban-industrial milieu. That milieu is central to the concerns of what might be called social psychoanalytic theory, particularly in the case of Marcuse, as Richard King points out in his *Party of Eros*.[1] King traces Freud's influence on American social reform theory, particularly in the works of Reich, Paul Goodman, Marcuse, and Brown. He concentrates on post–World War II intellectual retrenchment, when "the demise of Marxism as a persuasive radical ideology was paralleled by the rise of Sigmund Freud's theories to prominence among postwar intellectuals."[2] Freud's theories were pressed into the service of contradictory ideologies, becoming on one hand "a set of stultifying and conventional pieties" used as "a rationale for the political and social status quo."[3] On the other hand, such radicalists as Marcuse and Brown are in the tradition of Reich, who attempted to unite political and social radicalism. Of the three, Marcuse appears at first glance to be least like Blake and Reich most like him, Norman Brown's specific indebtedness to Blake notwithstanding. According to my reading, however, the correspondence is exactly reversed with regard to Marcuse and Reich.

Sexual liberation, and particularly the liberation of women, is at the core of Reich's theory and practice in and following *The Sexual Revolution*.[4] Sexual repression is the single villain of

Reich's system, and in this respect, Reich and Blake are loosely united. My use of Blake to expand upon the core of social implications in Freud's works on culture and society has some degree of commonality with Reich's argument that Freud did not carry his own analysis of cultural regression far enough into the arena of social reform. Reich's analysis of Freudian theory is often penetrating, and easy to underrate in the wake of Reich's later theoretical and clinical excesses. I ultimately agree with Reich's perceptions of the limitations of Freud, who remained, in Reich's words, "a middle class cultural philosopher."[5] But my agreements with Reich, and my acknowledgment of his parallels to Blake's social psychology, are superficial in comparison with my sense of his distance from both Freud and Blake in the most fundamental respect: as Juliet Mitchell documents in detail, Reich's thought constitutes a functional denial of unconscious mental life.[6] His *Character Analysis* clarifies the increasingly narrow and eventually monomaniac focus of Reichian "psychoanalysis." The neurotic patient must merely "establish a satisfactory genital sex life."[7] The ideal "genital character" is to achieve mental health through repeated and explosive orgasm. Political and economic oppression could not be maintained in an orgasmic society. Reich's emphasis on the "moral" value of the "natural," his equation of "sexual" and "genital," and his rejection of the theory of dual drives divide him not only from Freud but from useful comparison with Blake. Finally, it is difficult to comment seriously on Reich's later attempts to unite biophysics with politics, culminating in his discovery that the "orgone," the basic electrical energy unit, discharges "according to definite physical laws."[8] Ironically, Reich's claim to objective natural science status united his theory almost perversely with that of Freud, whose lifelong attempt to win for psychoanalysis the status of a natural science was also unsuccessful.

Marcuse's revisionist psychoanalysis is far more complex than Reich's. Marcuse's relationship to classicism, Marx, Hegel, and Heidegger defies any effort at brief summary, but his use of Freud nevertheless remains accessible. The core of Marcuse's revisionism is his supposition of an advanced technological and industrial society in which to apply radical social reform through psychoanalytic theory. This milieu seems to preclude the possibility of deep similarities between Marcuse and Blake; the industrial revolution was just beginning in Blake's world, while in Marcuse's, the industrializing process has produced conditions Blake could not have foreseen. So it would appear—but Blake's analysis of labor is strikingly similar to Marcuse's. For Blake and Marcuse, labor is a fundamental mediating activity. "Alienated labor" characterizes culture at the present time, according to Marcuse. The opposite of alienated labor is variously defined by Marcuse at different times in his career as the absence of labor, transformed labor, and creative imagination and its products— that is, art. Marcuse wavered in his original conviction that the abolition of alienated labor was likely to be actualized, and he modified his theories extensively after the original publication of *Eros and Civilization: A Philosophical Inquiry into Freud*. He remained convinced, as did Blake, that "the methodological sacrifice of libido, its rigidly enforced deflection to socially useful activities and expressions, *is* culture."[9] Marcuse did not, however, agree with Freud's "identification of civilization with repression." According to Marcuse, the seemingly deterministic interrelations between "freedom and repression, productivity and destruction, domination and progress," constitute not the basic principles of civilization, but rather "a specific historical organization of human existence."[10] The "reality principle" now coincides with its present manifestation, which Marcuse calls the "performance principle," but the two are not synoymous.[11] Marcuse denies, from within a rereading of Freud's own works, Freud's denial of "the historical possibility of a nonrepressive civilization." Instead, Marcuse theorizes that "the very achievements of repressive civilization" will "create the preconditions for the gradual abolition of repression.[12]

Marcuse's almost visionary theory is dependent on his early conjecture that the technological society, having wrung generations of its members dry and dead, will ultimately provide the leisure in which absence of labor, or play, or art, will reconstitute both consciousness and unconsciousness. Blake's vision of a new civilization based on art and love (or redemption effected through fall, or regeneration through generation) is not fleshed out with the particulars that arise from Marcuse's historical vantage point and from his fusion of classical, European, and American thought; but Blake foresaw both the dismal actuality of alienated labor which Marcuse analyzes and the possibility of transforming work into art and labor into love. Marcuse's ideal civilization of creativity, imagination, and love is a twentieth-century version of what Blake calls Eternity in his later "prophecies." Marcuse's analysis of the "performance principle" as historical stage that may be transcended corresponds to Blake's mythopoetic cycles and "states."

The deepest parallel between Marcuse and Blake occurs in Marcuse's discussions of imagination, or what Freud called "phantasy."

> Phantasy (imagination) retains the structure and the tendencies of the psyche prior to its organization by the reality, prior to its becoming an 'individual' set off against other individuals. . . . Imagination preserves the 'memory' of the subhistorical past when the life of the individual was the life of the genus, the image of the immediate unity between the universal and the particular under the rule of the pleasure principle. In contrast, the entire subsequent history of man is characterized by the destruction of this original unity. . . . Imagination envisions the reconciliation of the individual with the whole, of desire with realization, of happiness with reason.[13]

"Reason" is a privileged term in Marcusean thought, which seems to present a barrier to analogues with Blake, for whom "the reasoning power in man" is the conflation of all self-destructive principles. But in fact, Marcuse's "reason" is Blake's "intellect." What passes for reason, according to Marcuse, is merely "the rationality of the performance principle," defined as "an instrument of constraint, of instinctual suppression."[14] Marcuse's "Great Refusal" of the imagination to "accept as final the limitations imposed upon freedom and happiness by the reality principle," its "refusal to forget what *can be*," is also Blake's refusal to "cease from mental fight," until "we have built Jerusalem in England's green and pleasant land."

Through Schiller, Kant, and a reinterpretation of classical idealist aesthetics, Marcuse defines a redeemed and redemptive version of reason as counter to what he calls "the tyranny of reason." Marcuse's delineation of the historical separation of reason and the senses and his call for their reconciliation through art and love are analogous to Blake's differentiation of "negations" and proper "contraries." Marcuse's suggestion for "regression" from civilized rationality to "libidinal rationality" meets Blake's poetry at so many points that reading the last third of *Eros and Civilization* is like reading a secular, philosophical version of Blake's *Milton* and *Jerusalem*.[15] Unlike Reich, and like Blake, Marcuse opts for transformation of libido away from "sexuality constrained under genital supremacy" and toward "erotization of the entire personality."[16] Marcuse's analysis of Freudian sublimation and his revision of the concept is almost precisely what the reader will find attributed to Blake in the pages that follow.[17]

The single qualification on what I perceive as a radical similarity between Marcuse and Blake emerges from Marcuse's reading of Freud's dual drive theory. For Marcuse, Freudian theory represents "the most irrefutable indictment of Western civilization—and at the same time the most unshakable defense of this civilization."[18] (I agree with Marcuse, as my own reading of Freud will make clear.) Attempting to save psychoanalysis from itself, Marcuse finds the reconciliation of Eros and Thanatos in a transformation of the Nirvana principle. In the mythic images of Orpheus and Narcissus, "static triumphs over dynamic" in such a way that pleasure is redeemed, death absorbed, time halted.[19] Marcuse's reification of the static and passive conflicts with Blake's similarly strong reification of energy and activity. But the end result is the same in both systems, as any reader of Blake will recognize after reading this excerpt from Marcuse on Orpheus and Narcissus:

Theirs is the image of joy and fulfillment; the voice which does not command, but sings; the gesture which offers and receives; the deed which is peace and ends the labor of conquest; the liberation from time which unites man with God, man with nature. . . . They recall the experience of a world which is not to be mastered and controlled but to be liberated—a freedom that will release the powers of Eros now bound in the repressed and petrified forms of man and nature. . . . The song of Orpheus breaks the petrification, moves the forest and the rocks—but moves them to partake in joy. . . . Orpheus is the archetype of the poet as *liberator* and *creator*. In his person, art, freedom, and culture are eternally combined. He is the poet of redemption, . . . not through force but through song.[20]

The culmination of Blake's *Milton* and *Jerusalem* are Marcuse's song of Orpheus, in which man and god, subject and object, are reconciled: "All Human Forms identified even Tree Metal Earth & Stone" (*Jerusalem* 99:57).

Norman O. Brown's *Life against Death* and *Love's Body* tantalizingly play (in the best senses) with the synthesis of Blake and Freud I endeavor to accomplish here. *Love's Body* repeatedly evokes both Blake and Freud, along with a veritable multitude of other poets and philosophers. Brown's identification of man as "a slave in love with his own chains" and his consequent emphasis on revolution of consciousness as an individual task to be accomplished within mind and body unite his view of the human psyche with Blake's.[21] Similarly, the "fall" from polymorphous perversity, or whole-body eroticism, is rooted in Blake as well as in other thinkers Brown credits, literary and philosophical. Brown's emphasis on the flight from death is more explicit than Blake's, though it in no way conflicts with Blake. Brown's ideal image of oneness unobstructed by dualism, however, is the child at the mother's breast, an image fraught with ambivalence for Blake. Brown's Dionysian body ego, which draws no distinction between self and other or between life and death, ultimately goes beyond Blake's constant protection of "Minute Particulars," even though the redeemed and integrated body partakes of Blake's ideal perhaps as much as Brown's. The theological dimension of Brown's thought and the poetics of his body psychology are always phrased in terms borrowed directly from and credited to Blake. "The fall is the Fall into Division of the one universal man." One may open almost any page of *Love's Body* and find Blake in Brown: "The prototype of all opposition or contrariety is sex."[22] It could be argued that although Brown credits Blake extensively, he still credits him not enough. "The shadow of the lost object becomes the nucleus of the ego; a shade, a spectre."[23] This phrasing, only one example of many, is probably borrowed directly from Blake. "A fiery consummation. Truth is a blaze. Error, or Creation, will be Burned up. It is burnt up the Moment Men cease to behold it." "Everything is holy. . . . Infinity in a grain of sand."[24] One is sometimes on the verge of thinking that Brown *is* Blake. Random quotation does not do justice to Brown's richly textured book, but it is in keeping with both the spirit and the letter of *Love's Body*; anecdotal, aphoristic synthesis is Brown's method of presentation, and perhaps the major strength of his style, which compels through poetry as much as through argument. But since it is Brown's intention to get beyond analysis to radical integration, a reader's desire to find systematic analysis will be thwarted, as perhaps it should be in such an undertaking.

The only point at which I find Brown deficient, in terms of his goals for himself and his reader in awakening to a redeemed body, is in his handling of sexual dialectic, whose significance he announces but finally does not develop. Although he does not exclude the female and the feminine, the consciousness from which he writes is explicitly masculine. In both Brown and Marcuse, according to Richard King, "men and women become Man in general, while sexual identity and differentiation receive little mention."[25] Of the three thinkers discussed here for their relationship to my reading of Freud through Blake through Freud, Reich is the only one who emphasized the implications of sexual dialectic. Ironically, as King points out, "Reich personally was guilty of the most blatant sexual double standard, and abhorred all deviations from genital sexuality."[26] The issue of feminine psychology and sexual dialectic is the major focus toward which my reading of Blake and Freud tends, and it is this that most clearly differentiates my work from that of Reich, Marcuse, and Brown. Blake's theories on feminine psychology represent an advance on Freud's, even if the chronology is ironically inverted. (I acknowledge my own biases by using this phraseology.)

The idea that Blake is "better" than Freud on the subject of feminine psychology is, by itself, not really new. But the ways in which Blake approached *normative* psychic processes in the female—as differentiated from his portrayal of female characters or his delineation of an ideal for masculine/feminine dialectic—is still unexplored, or at least greatly confused. References to anima and animus, and to psychic androgyny as Blake's ideal, arc limitedly useful, but approaches that depend on this terminology are usually as much wrong as right.[27] Filtering Blake through Jung ultimately tends to fuzz both of them into a lovely androgynous blur that can obscure Blake's contributions to sexual psychology. I regard those contributions as significant for social and academic feminism in the 1980s—not because Blake rescues feminism from Freud, but because he brings feminism back to Freud.

I conclude this book with a rereading of Freud's theories on feminine psychology. I regard Blake as an advance on Freud in this respect, as I have said, but Blake's theories on feminine psychology are classically Freudian in ways that will become clear. Although I am a feminist, my conclusions are not particularly compatible with those of feminist psychologists, who have, for the most part, rejected Freud.[28] My conclusions are, however, compatible with those of some feminist psychoanalytic theorists, particularly Juliet Mitchell.

Blake and Freud is as much a reconsideration of Freud as it is of Blake, and ultimately not at Freud's expense. Blake and Freud illuminate each other. Blake needs Freud to clarify Blake's contributions to psychology in accessible terms, just as Freud needs Blake to expand the potentials already inherent in the psychoanalytic model of mind. I have had to "misread" both Blake and Freud, in some ways, to accomplish my purpose. My own anxiety of influence, as critic, will be evident. There is one other critic whose work synthesizes Blake and Freud, and my reasons for not citing Harold Bloom probably have something in common with Bloom's own judicious restriction of references to Blake in his *Anxiety of Influence* and *Map of Misreading*. Bloom's work begins at a level of sophistication that assumes the synthesis of Blake and Freud. The assumption is sufficiently implicit that Bloom does not mention it, and confines his Blake allusions to epigrams and dependent clauses. Indeed, one need not understand the interrelationship of Blake and Freud to comprehend Bloom's critical theories; Bloom supplies his readers with other, equally significant ways to confront the issues he presents. Although it is not his primary concern to synthesize Blake and Freud, it is fair to say that Bloom's work accomplishes part of the integration I propose here. Our purposes, however, are quite different—nearly, perhaps, opposite. At the risk of being somewhat unfair to Bloom's work and to my own, I would say that Bloom's primary purpose is to demonstrate that prophecy is mimetic; mine is to demonstrate that mimesis is prophetic.

Finally, I also intend *Blake and Freud* as a new kind of psychoanalytic literary criticism, as distinct from a contribution to psychoanalytic theory. Leo Bersani's *Baudelaire and Freud* may be said to begin this overdue venture; that is, Bersani's book is "an experimental working out of a hypothesis concerning a particular form of intertextuality."[29] With the significant exception of "transactive" or "response-centered criticism," I agree with Bersani that psychoanalytic criticism "re-places the writer within the infantile sexual organization presumably indicated by his preferred symbols. Most psychoanalytic studies of literature have used the notion of fantasy as a means of *im*mobilizing the writer . . . in certain fixed desires or sexual scenarios."[30] Bersani's hypothesis concerns the mobility of fantasy and its potential for "explosive displacements," which he explores through Baudelaire and primarily post-Freudian psychoanalytic texts. My purpose is different from but complementary to Bersani's. Psychoanalysis is traditionally used to pin down authors and texts in the ways Bersani suggests; Freud himself initiated the tradition, and his followers have codified it. Freud was also the first to acknowledge that he was preceded in his psychological discoveries by the poets and artists whose works embody psychic phenomena. In *Blake and Freud*, I pursue this truth, in an effort to transform further the relationship between psychoanalytic and literary texts. I hope thereby to free both kinds of texts, rather than to bind them.

1. Opposition Is True Friendship

Opposition is true friendship.
—William Blake

But opposition is not necessarily enmity; it is merely misused and made an occasion for enmity.
—Sigmund Freud

Milton and Urizen, with five senses or daughters. From William Blake, *Milton*, Plate 18 (1804). Relief etching. Library of Congress, Rosenwald Collection.

Only the line drawn between two apparently opposing points defines and positions them. Opposition occurs within the most intimate connection; all adversary relationships are antagonistic and complementary. To oppose can be to complete. In this sense, Blake on the left opposes Freud on the right. Freud on the right opposes Blake on the left.

O what is life & what is Man. O what is
  Death? Wherefore
Are you my Children, natives in the
  Grave to where I go
Or are you born to feed the hungry
  ravenings of Destruction
To be the sport of Accident! to waste
  in Wrath & Love, a weary
Life, in brooding cares & anxious
  labours, that prove but chaff.
        [*Jerusalem* 24:12–16]

No individual can keep these Laws,
  for they are death
To every energy of man, and forbid
  the springs of life.
        [*Jerusalem* 31:11–12]

O! father & mother, if buds are nip'd,
And blossoms blown away,
And if the tender plants are strip'd
Of their joy in the Springing day,
By sorrow and cares dismay,

How shall the summer arise in joy
Or the summer fruits appear
Or how shall we gather what griefs
  destroy

It is very far from my intention to express an opinion on the value of human civilization. I can at least listen without indignation to the critic who is of the opinion that when one surveys the aims of cultural endeavor and the means it employs, one is bound to come to the conclusion that the whole effort is not worth the trouble, and that the outcome of it can only be a state of affairs which the individual will be unable to tolerate. My impartiality is made all the easier by my knowing very little about these things. One thing only do I know for certain and that is that man's judgments of value follow directly his wishes for happiness—that, accordingly, they are an attempt to support his illusions with arguments. I should find it very understandable if someone were to point out the obligatory nature of the course of human

31

Or bless the mellowing year,
When the blasts of winter appear.
                ["The School Boy"]

... they accumulate
A world in which Man is by his Nature
   the Enemy of Man,
In pride of Selfhood unwieldy
   stretching out into NonEntity
Generalizing Art & Science til Art &
   Science is Lost.
                [*Jerusalem* 38:52–54]

Prophets in the modern sense of the
word have never existed. Jonah was
no prophet in the modern sense for
his prophecy of Nineveh failed Every
honest man is a Prophet he utters his
opinion both of private & public matters.... [Annotations to Richard
Watson's *Apology for the Bible*]

Desire Still pines but for one
Cooling Drop and tis Deny'd.
      ["Then She bore Pale desire ..."]

civilization and were to say, for
instance, that the tendencies to
a restriction of sexual life or to
the institution of a humanitarian ideal at the expense of
natural selection were developmental trends which cannot
be averted or turned aside and
to which it is best for us to yield
as though they were necessities
of nature. I know, too, the objection that can be made against
this, to the effect that in the
history of mankind, trends such
as these, which were considered
insurmountable, have often
been thrown aside and replaced
by other trends. Thus I have
not the courage to rise up before my fellow men as a prophet, and I bow to their reproach that I can offer them no
consolation: for at bottom that
is what they are all demand-
ing—the wildest revolution-
aries no less than the most
virtuous believers. [From the
last page of *Civilization and Its
Discontents*][1]

Freud's life and career
were monuments to the tensions this passage describes.
His disclaimer of the inclination and the requisite
knowledge to hold an opinion on the value of civilization must elicit a smile from
any reader of the preceding
hundred-page indictment

I wander thro' each chartered street,
Near where the charter'd Thames
   does flow.
And mark in every face I meet
Marks of weakness, marks of woe.

In every cry of Every Man,
In every Infants cry of fear,
In every voice: in every ban,
The mind-forg'd manacles I hear
                 ["London"]

... O perverse to thyself, contrarious
To thy own purposes. ...
             [*Jerusalem* 88:26-27]

It indeed appear'd to
Reason as if Desire was cast out. ...
[*The Marriage of Heaven and Hell*,
                Plate 5]

Excess in youth is necessary to
Life. [Annotations to Bacon]

of civilization for a job not well done. *Civilization and Its Discontents* traces the fundamental antagonism between the demands of human instinct and of civilization, and concludes that the means of civilization are at odds with its declared ends. The far-be-it-from-me stance of the passage above is best taken with a grain of saltpeter, for it represents Freud's own capitulation to the "necessities of nature."

Throughout the text of *Civilization and Its Discontents*, Freud in fact expressed both of the first two opinions he projects to imagined critics at the conclusion of the book: that indeed civilization is not worth the trouble, and (not "or") that we are stuck with it. The only opinion he did not permit himself is the third and consolatory one. I mean "permit himself" literally. He calls for a reconstitution of civilization through modifications of sexual morality, but he knows the demand is born of a wish he expressed elsewhere as the inclusion of "individual

All the infant Loves & Graces were
 lost, for the mighty Hand
Condens'd his Emanations into hard
 opake substances
And his infant thoughts & desires,
 into cold, dark cliffs of death.
His hammer of gold he siezd; and his
 anvil of adamant.
He siez'd the bars of condens'd
 thoughts to forge them. . . .
          [*Jerusalem* 8:43-44; 9:1-4]

. . . What seems to Be: Is: To those to
 whom
It seems to Be, & is productive of the
 most dreadful
Consequences to those to whom
 it seems to Be . . .
          [*Jerusalem* 32:50-53]

The Suns Light when he unfolds it
Depends on the Organ that beholds it.
 [*The Gates of Paradise*, Frontispiece]

happiness among the aims of cultural development."[2] The only way he can pretend to the "impartiality" he values so highly as the father of a fledgling science struggling for legitimacy is to disclaim value judgments, precisely because his science had discovered what he clarifies in the next sentence: such judgments always follow wishes, and attempt to support illusions with arguments. It is, he says, the one thing he knows for certain.

Among the things he does not say here, but which he certainly knew, is that the dilemma created by the antagonism of impulse and natural necessity was his own. Instead, he attempted to describe it "objectively," as if he did not have a personal stake in it. Freud began by testing the validity of psychoanalysis in the depths of his own personality as well as in those of his patients. But he ended by absenting himself from the arena. He argued eloquently for the realignment of civilized morality to

By demonstration, man alone can
    live, and not by faith.
My mountains are my own, and I will
    keep them to myself: . . .
So spoke Albion in jealous fears . . .
            [*Jerusalem* 4:28–29, 33]

How do you know but ev'ry Bird that
    cuts the airy way,
Is an immense world of delight, clos'd
    by your senses five?
[*The Marriage of Heaven and Hell*, "A
            Memorable Fancy"]

allow for human happiness, but he vigorously denied it to himself, opting instead for the "higher achievements" of sublimation, whose ultimate efficacy he questioned in the theoretical works.

By this process, Freud attempted to purge himself of illusions. He sustained his own illusion of impartiality and objectivity—the illusion of illusionlessness—out of great need and at great cost. The need grew out of the wish to establish psychoanalysis as a science, and, of course, out of deeper wishes best left to the biographer. The cost was hope. Or, to use his own word here, consolation. Science cannot trust to illusions, in Freud's view. It must stick to the facts. And the facts, devoid of consolation, hope, or vision, are grim. "Science betokens the most complete renunciation of the pleasure-principle of which our minds are capable," he wrote in 1910 as an aside in another discussion.[3] (This from the man who demonstrated that excessive re-

For Art & Science cannot exist but in
minutely organized Particulars . . .
[*Jerusalem* 55:62]

Every Mans Wisdom is peculiar to his
own Individuality
[*Milton* 4:8]

One Law for the Lion & Ox is
Oppression
[*The Marriage of Heaven and Hell*, "A
Memorable Fancy"]

If the Spectator could Enter into these
Images in his Imagination approach-
ing them on the Fiery Chariot of his
Contemplative Thought, if he could
Enter into Noahs Rainbow or into his
bosom or Could make a Friend &
Companion of one of these Images of
wonder . . . then would he meet the
Lord in the Air & then he would be
happy. . . . ["A Vision of the Last
Judgment"]

Those who restrain desire, do so because theirs is weak enough to be restrained. [*The Marriage of Heaven
and Hell*, Plate 5]

nunciation of the pleasure
principle is the root of all
evil.) Freud taught his
readers carefully to examine
"asides," and his own reveal
a great deal about the style
and the consequences of his
own system's compromises
with instinctual gratification.

Happiness, in the reduced
sense in which we recognize it as
possible, is a problem of the
economics of the individual's
libido. . . . Every man must find
out for himself in what particular fashion he can be saved.
. . . It is a question of how
much real satisfaction he can
expect to get from the external
world, how far he is led to making himself independent of it,
and, finally, how much strength
he feels he has for altering the
world to suit his wishes.[4]

Freud's own "particular
fashion" of salvation—and
therefore the particular
fashion offered by his methodology—must be conse-
sequent upon his assessment
of man's relationship to the
external world. Elsewhere in
the same essay is one such
assessment in terms of the
"three sources from which
our suffering comes":

... I assert for My self that I do not behold the Outward Creation & that to me it is hindrance & not Action it is as the Dirt upon my feet no part of Me. What [?] it will be Questioned [,] When the Sun rises do you not see a round Disk of fire somewhat like a Guinea [?] O no no I see an Innumerable company of the Heavenly host.... ["A Vision of the Last Judgment"]

I have been very near the Gates of Death & have returned very weak & an Old Man feeble & tottering, but not in Spirit & Life, not in The Real Man The Imagination which Liveth for Ever. In that I am stronger & stronger as this Foolish Body decays. [Blake to George Cumberland, April 12, 1827]

...he has made This World the Foundation of All & the Goddess Nature.... [Inscription on Design 7 of Blake's illustrations for Dante, "Hell Canto 4"]

... the superior power of nature, the feebleness of our own bodies, and the inadequacy of the regulations which adjust the mutual relationships of human beings in the family, the state, and society. In regard to the first two sources, our judgment cannot hesitate long. It forces us to acknowledge those sources of suffering and submit to the inevitable. We shall never completely master nature; and our bodily organism, itself a part of that nature, will always remain a transient structure with a limited capacity for adaptation and achievement.[5]

All of Freud's discussions of man's belief in the Fates apply to his own system. Nature is his God as well, if by God is meant the ultimate power and the immortal force toward which the mortal must tend. Psychoanalysis does not and cannot stand outside of the trends it anatomizes. Only the third source of suffering admits of hope, but it too is subject to the sternest qualifications. However much he wanted the world altered, Freud's perception of human history and his clinical experience did not en-

And this is the manner of the Sons of
    Albion . . .
They take the Two Contraries which
    are calld Qualities, with which
Every Substance is clothed, they name
    them Good & Evil [.]
From them they make an Abstract,
    which is a Negation
Not only of the Substance from which
    it is derived,
A murderer of its own Body: but also
    a murderer
Of every Divine Member . . .
                    [*Jerusalem* 10:7–13]

. . . a creeping skeleton
With lamplike eyes watching around
    the frozen marriage bed.
        [*Visions of the Daughters of Albion*]

Enitharmon nursd her fiery child in
    the dark deeps

courage him to trust the likelihood that civilization would change very much or very soon. The improbability of significant transformation is the thesis of *Civilization and Its Discontents*. That is why he had to decline the role of a prophet of hope. He repeatedly called, ironically prophet-like, for the alterations of sexual morality which he knew were so desperately needed. But his explorations of the human personality disclosed another kind of "unconquerable nature" in the fabric of psychic constitution, which he variously named the compulsion to repeat, the aggressive instincts, and the death instinct.[6] Though Freud never counseled despair, he must often have felt it; or perhaps by banishing hope he also banished despair.

But the reasons Freud denied himself and us the consolations of the prophet are the deeper products of his system. The feeling of hope is a derivative of a repressed and prototypical hope—that is, wish—which

Sitting in darkness. over her Los
  mourned in anguish fierce. . . .
. . . Los beheld the ruddy boy
Embracing his bright mother &
  beheld malignant fires
In his young eyes discerning plain
  that Orc plotted his death . . .
    [*The Four Zoas* 59:25–26; 60:7–9]

For man has closed himself up, till he
  sees all things thro' narrow chinks
  of his cavern.
    [*The Marriage of Heaven and Hell,*
                Plate 14]

Then come home my children, the
  sun is gone down
And the dews of night arise
Your spring & your day, are wasted in
  play
And your winter and night in
  disguise.
           ["Nurse's Song"]

is itself literally hopeless: sexual union with the parent. In order to play by his own rules, Freud was bound to view hope or consolation in these terms. Every "higher" human achievement or sensibility is the product of the repression and sublimation of "baser" motivations that are in fact the ground of being in Freud's psychoanalytic system.

The ultimate result is the shrinking of possibility. Freud thus advocated human happiness while he was absolutely compelled to acknowledge that "the programme of becoming happy . . . cannot be fulfilled."[7] The language of Freud's psychoanalysis is full of deterministic prohibitions and commands. In the passage above, our judgment "cannot hesitate." It "forces us" to "submit." Nature is "superior" in "power." Our bodies are "feeble" and "transient," and "limited."

But the language of compulsion is not limited to our enforced submissions. Even if happiness is impossible, "we must not—indeed we

For Los said: Tho my Spectre is
   divided: as I am a Living Man
I must compell him to obey me
   wholly: that Enitharmon may not
   Be lost. . . .
. . . O Enitharmon!
I will compell my Spectre to obey: I
   will restore to thee thy Children.
                [*Jerusalem* 17:16-20]

And because I am happy, & dance &
   sing,
They think they have done me no
   injury.
               ["The Chimney Sweeper"]

I must Create a System, or be enslav'd
   by another Mans
I will not Reason & Compare: my
   business is to Create
               [*Jerusalem* 10:20-21]

cannot—give up our efforts to bring it nearer to fulfillment."[8] The use of "cannot" here is far more than a rhetorical plea that we not give up the ship. We "cannot" in the sense that we are compelled to search for happiness because we do so instinctively. It is our literal fate. And it is an effort doomed to failure.

Freud's necessarily truncated ideal became advantageous compromise. But the compromise was itself another ideal fiction that was seldom advantageous and always compromising. Freud's discovery of these facts of human history and individual psychic life put him in a difficult situation. To adopt a Freudian-style analogy, it is as though he were both slaveholder and abolitionist—or better, perhaps, slave and abolitionist, with this twist: he kept himself in bondage by inventing a system that became his own harsh master. He cried, "Let my people go!" but his system said that all people are born in chains and must die in chains.

"Thus I have not the courage . . . " What he really means by courage is optimistic foolhardiness. ". . . and I bow to their reproach." The reproach is that of the child Freud knew every man to be, and Freud is the world-weary father who no longer deals in dreams and fairy tales. "I can offer them no consolation." Freud responded to the hostile reception of *Beyond the Pleasure Principle* by saying that "little children do not like it."[9] The reproach has the same content as the little girl's resentment of the mother who "has not given her a proper genital."[10] It is the protest of powerlessness. Freud exposed man's powerlessness before the forces of nature and his own inner life, and he anticipated that men would resent it, and blame him for their position as children blame their parents. And, of course, they were right. But in this case, Freud would have none of it. The unspoken content is, then: "I have renounced my wishes because they are all illusions. Though all men

O little Cloud the virgin said, I charge
   thee tell to me,
Why thou complainest not when in
   one hour thou fade away:
Then we shall seek thee but not find;
   ah Thel is like to Thee.
I pass away. yet I complain, and no
   one hears my voice.
                    [*The Book of Thel*, Plate 3]

Jerusalem is not! her daughters are
   indefinite . . .
                    [*Jerusalem* 4:27]

But the perturbed Man away turns
    down the valleys dark, saying
Phantom of the over heated brain!
    shadow of immortality!
                    [*Jerusalem* 4:22–24]

Go! tell the human race ...
That an Eternal life awaits the worm
    of sixty winters
In an allegorical abode where
    existence hath never come.
                    [*Europe* 6:5–8]

If it were not for the Poetic or Prophetic character the Philosophic &
Experimental would soon be the ratio
of all things, & stand still unable to do
other than repeat the same dull round
over again.   [Conclusion, *There Is No
Natural Religion (a)*]

are children, I am not. I am a
father, I am my own father,
I am the father of psychoanalysis, I am impartial
and objective and immune
to hopeless hopes, and
I will make no value judgments that would reveal ves-
tigial wishes. Prophets truck
in illusions, unless they are
only prophets of doom.
Therefore I am not a
prophet."

The "wildest revolution-
aries" and the "most
virtuous believers" are at
bottom the same. The revolutionary demands consolation in the form of hope for
liberty in an earthly future.
The virtuous believer de-
mands it in a spiritual future. Both are the futures of
illusions. Freud allies himself safely with the past, as
the only thing that is known.
Or, rather, it is known that
the future will be very like
the past and is determined
by it. There is, indeed, little
room for consolation.

But "I have not the cour-
age" is genuine as well as
false modesty. Freud greatly
admired courage, however
obliged he was to interpret

...and the restrainer or reason usurps its place & governs the unwilling. And being restrained it by degrees becomes passive till it is only the shadow of desire. [*The Marriage of Heaven and Hell,* Plate 5]

The man who holds miracles to be ceased puts it out of his own power to ever witness one.... Is it a greater miracle to feed five thousand men with five loaves than to overthrow all the armies of Europe with a small pamphlet [?] [On Thomas Paine, in Annotations to Richard Watson's *Apology for the Bible*]

Look over the events of your own life & if you do not find that you have both done such miracles & lived by such you do not see as I do.... How can Paine the worker of miracles ever doubt Christs in the above sense of the word miracle [?] But how can Watson ever believe the above sense of a miracle [,] who considers it as an arbitrary act of the agent upon an unbelieving patient. [Annotations to Richard Watson's *Apology for the Bible*]

its etiology in terms of instincts that were not intrinsically admirable. I think it safe to say he wished he could wish, and thereby hope, for consolation. The refusal to rise as a prophet is, after all, a reluctance to predict absolute doom.

One of the sharpest ironies in this passage is that Freud *was* a prophet, and in several senses. For many years, his was a voice crying out in the wilderness, which men refused to hear. He was misapprehended in the time-honored fashion of all prophets. Materialists rejected him for his alleged mysticism, idealists because they found him too materialistic. I suspect that Freud wrote this passage with a wry awareness of this irony. What I do not think he suspected was that he was himself both a wild revolutionary and a virtuous believer. Psychoanalysis made him a revolutionary, and then a virtuous believer.

What Freud ultimately denied is human liberty. We are not free because we are mortal slaves to nature and

SUCH VISIONS HAVE APPEARD TO ME
AS I MY ORDERD RACE HAVE RUN
JERUSALEM IS NAMED LIBERTY
AMONG THE SONS OF ALBION
                              [*Jerusalem* 26]

to our own natures. There was a way out, a means to liberty from within his own system, but it lay outside the tightly closed circle of natural destiny, so that Freud could not give it its due. It didn't fit, and he continually acknowledged that it didn't fit. Freud had the greatest admiration for imaginative artists, in praise of whose achievements he waxed nearly passionate. Little wonder: his system could not completely explain artistic process. Art and imagination became the only human phenomena toward which psychoanalysis bowed as a curious and wonderful "exemption" or "sanctuary" from the laws of nature that compelled human existence.

... but I the Fourth Zoa am also set
The Watchman of Eternity ...
    [The poet Los, in *Milton* 24:8–9]

The realm of imagination was evidently a "sanctuary" made during the painful transition from the pleasure principle to the reality principle in order to provide a substitute for the gratification of instincts which had to be given up in real life.[11]

A sanctuary made by whom? Or by what process? Freud

does not venture an answer.
And again:

Then Eno a daughter of Beulah took
  a Moment of Time
And drew it out to Seven thousand
  years with much care & affliction
And many tears & in Every year made
  windows into Eden
She also took an atom of space &
  opend its center
Into Infinitude & ornamented it with
  wondrous art
                    [*The Four Zoas* 9:9–13]

The region from which these
illusions arise is the life of the
imagination; at the time when
the development of the sense of
reality took place, this region
was expressly exempted from
the demands of reality testing
and was set apart for the fulfil-
ling of wishes which were difficult to carry out. At the head
of these satisfactions through
phantasy stands the enjoyment
of works of art.[12]

Expressly exempted by what
agency? The diction in both
cases implies volition and
motive power that protects
something immeasurably
dear against whatever might
destroy it. Freud was genuinely mystified by his
own response to art, by
something beyond the por-
tion of his response that he
could and did explain in analytic terms in essays on
Shakespeare, Dostoevsky,
Leonardo, and Michel-
angelo.[13] It was
something "beyond the
pleasure principle" in another direction from that
of aggression, pain, and
self-destruction.

Judge then of thy Own Self: thy
    Eternal Lineaments explore
What is Eternal & what Changeable?
    & what Annihilable!
The Imagination is not a State: it is the
    Human Existence itself

                [*Milton* 32:30–32]

His visage changd to darkness & his
    strong right hand came forth
To cast Ahania to the Earth he siezd
    her by the hair
And threw her from the steps of ice
    that froze around his throne

            [*The Four Zoas* 43:2–4]

There is a Moment in each Day that
    Satan cannot find
Nor can his Watch Fiends find it, but
    the Industrious find
This Moment & it multiply. & when it
    once is found
It renovates every Moment of the Day
    if rightly placed

            [*Milton* 35:42–46]

The two passages phrase the situation slightly differently. In the first Freud refers to a "substitute" for gratification, and juxtaposes it with "real life." In the second he seems to allow that imagination actually can fulfill, in some sense, those wishes. In "Formulations Regarding the Two Principles in Mental Functioning," he explored the question more fully. Ideally, the reality principle safeguards the pleasure principle; in fact, however, it generally inhibits the pleasure principle beyond the fictional ideal, rendering the individual partially or totally dysfunctional. But, he wrote, art reconciles the two principles in a "peculiar way":

The artist is originally a man who turns from reality because he cannot come to terms with the demand for renunciation of instinctual satisfaction as it is first made, and who then in phantasy-life allows full play to his erotic and ambitious wishes. But he finds a way of return from this world of phantasy back to reality; with his special gifts he moulds his phantasies into a new kind of reality, and men concede them a justification as valuable reflections of actual life. Thus by a certain path he actually becomes the hero, king, creator . . . he desired to be. . . . But this he can only attain because other men feel the same dissatisfaction as he with the renunciation demanded by reality, and because this dissatisfaction, resulting from the displacement of the pleasure-principle by the reality-principle, is itself a part of reality.[14]

The worship of God is Honouring his gifts in other men each according to his genius. [*The Marriage of Heaven and Hell*, "A Memorable Fancy"]

Vision or Imagination is a Representation of what Eternally Exists [,] Really and Unchangeably. ["A Vision of the Last Judgment"]

The diction is far more radical here. "A new kind of reality" is conceded to the artist's phantasies, not a substitute gratification. The artist "actually becomes" the hero, king, and creator Freud usually consigns to the primitive realm of myth and magic. The artist's world is one of wishes fulfilled for himself, and, by implication, for his audience. Their mutual "dissatisfaction" is their bond, and it is also the realistic medium through which the ideal is attained.

But Freud is always somewhat disarmed by the nature of the artist's "special gifts." His essays on litera-

"To God"
If you have formd a Circle to go into
Go into it yourself & see how you
would do

[From the *Notebook*]

To see a World in a Grain of Sand
And a Heaven in a Wild Flower
Hold Infinity in the palm of your
hand
And Eternity in an hour
["Auguries of Innocence"]

ture and art are attempts to "explain to myself what their effect is due to." When he cannot find a satisfactory explanation, he says, "I am almost incapable of obtaining any pleasure. Some rationalistic, or perhaps analytic, turn of mind in me rebels against being moved by a thing without knowing why I am thus affected and what it is that affects me."[15] His interpretations offer explanation for sources of configurations and images that are accessible to psychoanalytic method. He discloses the mythic components, and uncovers events in the artist's life which illuminate why a certain theme or motif is chosen. Why, but not how. The essays on art and literature are curiously silent about poetic process, with one exception. In "The Relation of the Poet to Day-Dreaming," he compares the writer to the child at play. In the process of daydreaming, "past, present and future are threaded, as it were, on the string of the wish that runs through them all."[16] Everyone daydreams,

Seeking the Eternal which is always
present to the wise. . . .
[*The Four Zoas* 121:10]

but the child and the artist are professionals at it, while the normal adult has "regressed" to amateur status by progressing to maturity. One of those "special gifts," then, is the ability to break free of linear time. The "new kind of reality" he spoke of in "Two Principles in Mental Functioning" is, by implication, timeless. To "actually become" a hero or creator—both denizens of the past—the artist must have access to past and future in the present moment.

For one seeking Freud's best discussions of the special gifts and the way they are employed, the essays on art are not, oddly enough, the most fruitful source. In his relatively early essay "The Unconscious," Freud recapitulates the basics of psychoanalytic technique in the topographic model. Incoherent conscious acts are rendered intelligible by interpolation and inference of unconscious acts. Since the writer's or artist's access to the unconscious allows him to create that "new kind of reality," Freud's discussion

The desire of Man being Infinite the possession is Infinite & himself Infinite. [*There Is No Natural Religion (b)*, VII]

All Things Exist in the Human
   Imagination
                    [*Jerusalem* 69:25]

Negations are not Contraries:
   Contraries mutually Exist:
But Negations Exist Not: Exceptions
   & Objections & Unbeliefs
Exist not . . .
                    [*Jerusalem* 17:33–35]

There is a place where Contrarieties
   are equally True
This place is called Beulah, It is a
   pleasant lovely Shadow
Where no dispute can come. . . .
                    [*Milton* 30:1–3]

Beulah is evermore Created around
   Eternity; appearing
To the Inhabitants of Eden, around
   them on all sides.
                    [*Milton* 30:8–9]

of the unconscious is applicable to the artist.

The characteristics of the unconscious are based on wish impulses.

They are co-ordinate with one another, exist independently side by side, and are exempt from mutual contradiction. . . . There is in this system no negation, no dubiety, no varying degree of certainty: all this is only imported by the work of the censorship which exists between Ucs and Pcs.* . . . Intensity of cathexis is mobile in a far greater degree. . . . By the process of displacement one idea may surrender to another the whole volume of its cathexis; by that of condensation it may appropriate the whole cathexis of several other ideas. I have proposed to regard these two processes as distinguishing marks of the so-called *primary process* in the mind. . . . The processes of the system Ucs are timeless; i.e., they are not ordered temporally, are not altered by the passage of time, in fact bear no relation to time at all. . . . The processes of the Ucs are just as little related to reality. They are subject to the pleasure-principle.[17]

---

*Ucs = Unconscious; Pcs = Preconscious.

Energy is the only life and is from the Body and Reason is the bound or outward circumference of Energy.
Energy is Eternal Delight [*The Marriage of Heaven and Hell*, Plate 4]

How many have fallen there!
They stumble all night over bones of
  the dead;
And feel they know not what but
  care . . .
  ["The Voice of the Ancient Bard"]

The nature of the special gifts becomes clearer. The artist is blessed with a faulty censorship system. In his development, there has been a disturbance of the normal process by which we become mature and civilized. Cathexis (from the Greek for "I occupy") is used in analogy with electric charge to mean a concentration of energy in some particular direction. The artist can cathect energy freely and intensely through the displacement and condensation processes Freud originally applied to the mechanisms of dreaming. While ordinary men and women live in the world of consciousness (secondary process), ruled by a primary process that they little understand and to which they have very limited access, the artist has retained the ability to reconcile paradox (exemption from "mutual contradiction"), to be certain and to assert ("no negation, no dubiety"), and to escape time.

But unlike the "insane" person who is trapped in the

Eternity is in love with the prod-
uctions of time. [*The Marriage of
Heaven and Hell*, "Proverbs of Hell"]

He now saw from the outside what he
before saw & felt from within
[*Jerusalem* 8:25]

As a beautiful Veil so these Females
shall fold & unfold

power of the Ucs system and
cannot adapt to reality, the
artist reconciles the two
principles in the manner
that began this part of the
discussion. He passes freely
between and among plea-
sure and pain, reality and
fantasy, time and timelessness. And timelessness is
nothing more nor less than
the meaning of the word
"eternity."

For a further refinement
of this theory of art which
lay buried in Freud's major
works, I turn to *Totem and
Taboo*, in which Freud compares individual psychic development to the history of
culture. The psychic process
of projection, by which
thoughts, things, and ac-
tions are displaced "from
our inner perception into
the outer world and [are]
thereby detached from our
own person and attributed
to the other," forms the basis
of his analysis.[18]

The projection of inner perceptions to the outside is a primitive
mechanism which . . . also in-
fluences our sense perceptions
so that it normally has the
greatest share in shaping our

According to their will the outside
  surface of the Earth
An outside shadowy Surface
  superadded to the real Surface . . .
                    [*Jerusalem* 83:45–47]

All his Affections now appear
  withoutside . . .
                    [*Jerusalem* 19:17]

From every-one of the Four Regions
  of Human Majesty,
There is an Outside spread Without,
  & an Outside spread Within . . .
                    [*Jerusalem* 18:1–2]

. . . Envy Revenge & Cruelty
Which separated the stars from the
  mountains: the mountains from
  Man
And Left Man, a little grovelling Root,
  outside of Himself.
                    [*Jerusalem* 17:30–32]

outer world. Under conditions that have not yet been sufficiently determined, even inner perceptions of ideational and emotional process are projected outwardly, like sense perceptions, and are used to shape the outer world, whereas they ought to remain in the inner world.[19]

There seem to be two kinds of projection here. One is "normal" and is credited with the power actually to shape the outer world. The other is excessive with respect to the norm, and "ought to" remain internalized. Freud's underlying framework was, after all, the etiology of neurosis. In the projective process he saw not only man's mastery of the external world, but also his fear of it, and his inability to cope with what was inside him. Freud's view of human history, both collective and individual, compelled him to describe projection primarily in negative terms. That view also led him to adopt R. Taylor's definition of magic as the "mistaking [of] an ideal connection for a real one."[20] The perception

Wherefore in dreadful majesty &
  beauty outside appears
Thy Masculine from thy Feminine
  hardening against the heavens
To devour the Human!
                    [*Jerusalem* 79:70–72]

that projective process can shape the outer world might suggest that the outer world is malleable. Instead, Freud's belief in the inexorable reality of nature, of the given empirical world, made him emphasize man's tendency to *mis*shape the outer world, to the limited extent Freud thought it could be shaped at all. Freud gave the name "Omnipotence of Thought" to the principle that controls magic and defines projection. It is the basis of animism.

Animism is a system of thought; it gives not only the explanation of a single phenomenon, but makes it possible to comprehend the totality of the world. ... Writers maintain that in the course of time three such systems of thought, three great world systems came into being: the animistic (mythological), the religious and the scientific. Of these three, animism, the first system, is perhaps the most consistent and the most exhaustive, and the one which explains the nature of the world in its entirety.[21]

In fact, the survival of animistic thought is what psychoanalysis uncovered.

It forms "a complete theory of psychic concepts." In the wider sense, Freud calls it "the theory of spiritual beings in general." Nor does it survive only in superstition or in pathological states; Freud claims its existence in "living form, as the foundation of our language, our belief, our philosophy."[22] All this on the basis of mistaking the ideal for the real. Utilizing Freud's own rhetorical method of disingenuousness, I must say that this seems most peculiar. Perhaps a closer look at the developmental stages of these three systems of thought is needed.

In the animistic phase of culture and of the individual (narcissism), man ascribes omnipotence to himself. In the religious phase, which is analogous to the early phases of object finding in the individual, man cedes omnipotence to the gods. In the final stage, the scientific, there is "no longer any room for man's omnipotence; he has acknowledged his smallness and has submitted to death as to all other

The ancient Poets animated all sensible objects with Gods or Geniuses, calling them by the names and adorning them with the properties of woods, rivers, mountains, lakes, cities, nations, and whatever their enlarged & numerous senses could perceive.... Till a system was formed, which some took advantage of & enslav'd the vulgar by attempting to realize or abstract the mental deities from their objects; thus began Priesthood. Choosing forms of worship from poetic tales. And at length they pronounced that the Gods had ordered such things. Thus men forgot that All deities reside in the human breast. [*The Marriage of Heaven and Hell*, Plate 11] natural necessities in a spirit of resignation." The analogue in the individual person is the state of maturity, in which, having "renounced the pleasure-principle" and "adapted himself to reality," the person "seeks his object in the outer world."[23]

The forlorn phrasing of the scientific phase of culture sorts very oddly with the fact that it represented Freud's ideal. His ideal is formed of compromises with what he perceived as the "real." And the description of the scientific phase in the individual rings with Freud's approval of the normal outcome of ideal human development. Freud clearly regards this developmental process in progressive terms, though with the many qualifications that form the argument of *Civilization and Its Discontents.* The scientific phase is "higher" in qualitative terms for him. Freud understood man's need for the religious phase, but regarded it as yet another illusion by means of which man gives up the

. . . as in your own Bosom you bear
    your Heaven
And Earth, & all you behold, tho it
    appears Without it is Within
In your Imagination of which this
    World of Mortality is but a Shadow.
                    [*Jerusalem* 71:17–19]

Thou Mother of my Mortal part
With cruelty didst mould my Heart,
And with false self-decieving tears,
Didst bind my Nostrils Eyes & Ears.

Didst close my Tongue in senseless
    clay
And me to Mortal Life betray:
The Death of Jesus set me free,
Then what have I to do with thee?
                        ["To Tirzah"]

power that properly belongs to himself. In individual terms, the child should not remain in thrall to the parent, but must obtain mastery over those instincts and forces that would keep him forever dependent.

How is it, then, that this third and highest phase of culture does not increase man's power, but rather diminishes it, even annihilates it? From one point of view, Freud's analogy of cultural and individual development holds good throughout. But from another, it breaks down completely, and the two trends take literally opposite directions. He might, of course, have phrased what happens differently, thereby erasing the contradictions. He might have characterized the scientific stage as one in which man obtains mastery over the forces of nature and takes life into his own hands—and in fact, in other contexts he seemed to say exactly that, though always with qualifications that give the perception only limited validity.

All of the contradictions

Mental Things are alone Real what is Calld Corporeal Nobody Knows of its dwelling Place . . . ["A Vision of the Last Judgment"]

The Nature of Visionary Fancy or Imagination is very little Known & the Eternal nature & permanence of its ever Existent Images is considerd as less permanent than the things of Vegetative & Generative Nature. . . . ["A Vision of the Last Judgment"]

The Spectre is the Reasoning Power
    in Man; & when separated
From Imagination, and closing itself
    as in steel, in a Ratio
Of the Things of Memory [,] It thence
    frames Laws & Moralities
To destroy Imagination!
                    [*Jerusalem* 74:10-12]

These Gods are visions of the eternal attributes, or divine names, which, when erected into gods, become destructive to humanity. They ought to be the servants, and not the masters of man, or of society. ["A Descriptive Catalogue"]

arise, it seems to me, from Freud's restricted definition of the "real." He expanded the category of the real, it is true, to include noumena as well as phenomena. It might even be claimed that he made noumena the basis of phenomena by demonstrating that consciousness is only a small part of man's mental activity. But he applied what he learned about noumena *only to* phenomena, drawing a neat line that broke out of the tight circle only to return to it as the basis of the given. Here was his own repetition compulsion, his own "death instinct" at work, conservative, regressive, and repetitive.

He makes one important distinction in the discussion of animism and projection. I shall pursue its implications in order to suggest a way out of the circle. Magic is the technique of animism, and magic retains the full force of "Omnipotence of Thought." But animism has "ceded part of this omnipotence to spirits and thus has started on the way to form a religion."[24] Freud mentions a preanimistic system called animatism, which is a theory of general animation of all people and all things. He does not discuss it because it has no historical or psychic precedents. In other words, our knowledge of early culture does not extend to a time when man was not already on his way to a religion.

Once Man was occupied in
intellectual pleasures & energies
But now my soul is harrowd with grief
& fear....

[*Jerusalem* 68:65]

For All Things Exist in the Human
Imagination

[*Jerusalem* 69:25]

Many suppose that before the Creation All was Solitude & Chaos [.] This is the most pernicious Idea that can enter the Mind ... as it Limits All Existence ... ["A Vision of the Last Judgment"]

One way to grasp some of the import of animatism is to return to the two kinds of projection I inferred from Freud's passage quoted above. In the animatistic phase, then, the projection process actually shapes the outer world. To use the sacred and artistic terminology, it creates it. All things are animated by the human spirit, and are part of that human spirit. The reason that Freud can find no historical precedents for it, and can only posit it as a theory, is that it is simultaneous with creation. The second and later kind of projection has become a movement back and forth in which man has begun to credit his own creations with independent force and will, that is, to make them into gods.

Now Freud can provide an entrée back into the discussion of art. It is another of his "asides," stated and then dropped.

Only in one field has the omnipotence of thought been retained in our civilization, namely in art. In art alone, it still happens that man, consumed by his wishes, produces something similar to the gratification of these wishes, and this playing, thanks to artistic illusion, calls forth effects as if it were something real.[25]

"As if it were something real." But in others of his statements on art, that idea was omitted. I would like to exploit the omission as Freud has taught me to do, and pursue a theory of art that is possible from within the psychoanalytic system, one that offers the "consolation" Freud denied himself and us in *Civilization and Its Discontents*. Psychoanalysis contains the seed of hope and vision of which Blake's system was the harvest a century before.

Labour well the Minute Particulars, attend to the Little-ones:

[*Jerusalem* 55:51]

. . . so he who wishes to see a Vision, a
   perfect Whole
Must see it in its Minute Particulars [,]
   Organized. . .
                    [*Jerusalem* 91:20-21]

. . . He who enters into and discrimi-
nates most minutely the Manners &
Intentions [,] the Characters in all
their branches is the alone Wise or
Sensible Man & on this discrimination
All Art is founded.   ["A Vision of the
Last Judgment"]

Freud's clinical meth-
odology consisted of
reestablishing broken connections, revealing the fundamental reality hidden
beneath superficies and at-
tributing to them the utmost
significance. The first tenet
of the method was to pay
close attention to seemingly
insignificant details, to
throwaway comments and
asides. Freud's comments on
art in his theoretical texts are
his asides. The slightly different phrasings of the relationship of artistic "illusion"
to reality are crucial. Had he
been able to pay more attention to the implications of
"actually become" and "new
kind of reality" and "ex-
pressly exempted" and "ful-
filling of wishes," he might
have been able to find his
way out of the deterministic
trap that made him so obviously unhappy with his own
findings about human na-
ture. The man who proved
that so many of our realities
are illusions might have
been able to find that many
of our illusions are realities.

What Freud and his sys-
tem repressed, then, is the

. . . As the Reasoning Spectre
Stands between the Vegetative Man
    and his Immortal Imagination
And the Four Zoas clouded rage East
    & West & North & South
They change their situations, in the
    Universal Man.
                    [*Jerusalem* 32:23–26]

What are all the Gifts of the Spirit but
Mental Gifts [?] ["A Vision of the
Last Judgment"]

I know of no other Christianity and of
no other Gospel than the liberty both
of body and mind to exercise the Divine Arts of Imagination [.]   [Jerus-
alem 77]

I give you the end of a golden string,
Only wind it into a ball:
It will lead you in at Heavens gate,
Built in Jerusalem's wall.
                    [*Jerusalem* 77]

full significance of man's imaginative freedom, Blake's "fourth fold" of humanity, which he called Liberty. For Blake, it is literally the definition of being fully human, not an adjunct. Freud wrote that a "fragment" of the primitive belief in the omnipotence of thought lives on in our "reliance upon the power of the human spirit." That fragment provides psychoanalysis with new directions if its implications are followed out. "Spirit" is often a pejorative word for Freud, used disparagingly to connote illusion, primitivity, and man's ceding of his own authority to elusive and external forces whose sources he must learn to recognize in himself. But here he uses it as a term of approbation. Freud admired and loved the human spirit, and desired to set it free. It is that absolutely indomitable human spirit which produces great art, in Freud's view. After all his interpolations and interpretations were done with, there remained something

Is the Holy Ghost any other than an
Intellectual Fountain?
[*Jerusalem* 77]

All Human Forms identified even
Tree Metal Earth & Stone. . . .
[*Jerusalem* 99:1]

The Lamb of God has rent the Veil of
Mystery . . .
The Four Zoas 110:1]

irreducible in his response to art and imagination, something that did not admit of complete analysis, which he consequently put aside as exemption and sanctuary.

The artist is the pre-animist who animates everything he touches: stone, canvas, paper. His projections shape the outer world in positive rather than negative ways. When Freud wrote that the artist actually becomes the hero-king-creator, he was acknowledging this shaping power of the human imagination. The reality principle is thereby subject to, because created by, the artist. Through art, the reality principle reasserts its healthful function of protecting the pleasure principle, rather than subverting it. Art provides access to the fundamentally animatistic unconscious. The unconscious processes, rather than remaining the tyrants mysteriously veiled and unseen, are revealed and open. Psychoanalysis uncovered the unconscious, or the pri-

And a double vision is always with me.
With my inward Eye 'tis an old Man
    grey;
With my outward, a Thistle across my
    way.
[From a poem in a letter to Thomas
butts, November 22, 1802]

And did those feet in ancient time
Walk upon Englands mountains
    green:
And was the Holy Lamb of God
On Englands pleasant pastures seen!

And did the Countenance Divine,
Shine forth upon our clouded hills?
And was Jerusalem builded here,
Among these dark Satanic Mills?

mary process, and posited it as the source of energy and the motive power of conscious life. That power can manifest itself for good or evil. Art is one expression of the good, because it is released energy rather than repressed energy.

In this sense, then, magic is not the *mis*taking of an ideal connection for a real one at all. Rather, it is the *taking* of an ideal connection for a real, an appropriation that transforms the nature of reality; magic is the basis of metaphor. The metaphorical process is the primary process. It disregards time, space, and all other dissimilarities in favor of a unity it finds, or makes, that underlies diversity. It might be said of Freud that in regard to art and imagination, he mistook a real connection for an ideal one.

The animatism of art poses an alternative to the third and "highest" phase of cultural development, in which "there is no longer any room for man's omnipotence." Although art must be regarded partly as a re-

Bring me my Bow of burning gold:
Bring me my Arrows of desire:
Bring me my Spear: O clouds unfold!
Bring me my Chariot of fire!

I will not cease from Mental Fight
Nor shall my Sword sleep in my hand:
Till we have built Jerusalem
In Englands green & pleasant Land.
                              [*Milton*, Preface]

gressive trend in the psychoanalytic model, it restores man to mythic status *in a real sense*. Finally, art and imagination, still in analogy with animatism, make it possible to "comprehend the totality of the world."

The passage from *Civilization and Its Discontents* with which I began is not quite the final one in the book. In the last sentences, Freud muses on the relationship between Eros and Thanatos, and wonders if man can find a way to defeat self-destructive instinctual trends. He has just declined the prophet role, but now he calls for one himself. "And now it is to be expected that the other of the two 'Heavenly Powers,' eternal Eros, will make an effort to assert himself in this struggle with his equally immortal adversary."[26] Freud speaks here, as he so often does, in the voice of the poet-maker himself, half ironically and half seriously mythologizing the forces his theories attempt to demystify. Freud, the fair flower of the third-stage man, was also a con-

Urthona rises from the ruinous walls
In all his ancient strength to form the
 golden armour of science. . . .
The dark Religions are departed &
 sweet Science reigns
 [*The Four Zoas* 139:8–10]

Note. The Reason Milton wrote in
fetters when he wrote of Angels &
God, and at liberty when of Devils &
Hell, is because he was a true Poet and
of the Devils party without knowing
it.   [*The Marriage of Heaven and Hell*,
Plate 5]

Prayer is the Study of Art
Praise is the Practice of Art
 [Inscriptions for "The Laocoön"]

summate artist, as students of his work have always recognized. But far more fundamentally, the whole psychoanalytic system for which Freud was so determined to win the title of "science" was based on radical metaphor, analogy, and symbol. It was, and is, one of the most highly developed systems of symbolism ever devised, and one of the most radically metaphoric as well. More than that: it is not just based on radical metaphor. It *is* a radical metaphor. Freud's theoretical texts are monumental epics of mankind's creation and fall. They constitute the *Paradise Lost* of the twentieth century. The stuff of Freud's *Paradise Regained* might have manifested itself in the ways I have tried to describe, but instead it remained latent, that is, unwritten. If Freud had fully perceived just how fine a poet he really was, he might have seen that he could "actually become" a poet-prophet of that other kind of reality.

Freud's complaint about civilization was that it de-

... she who burns with youth and
   knows no fixed lot is bound
In spells of law to one she loaths: and
   must she drag the chain
Of Life in weary lust! must chilling
   murderous thoughts obscure
The clear heaven of her eternal
   spring? to bear the wintry rage
Of a harsh terror driv'n to
   madness. . . .
          [*Visions of the Daughters of Albion*,
                                    Plate 5]

Art & Science cannot exist but by
   Naked Beauty displayd
                    [*Jerusalem* 32:49]

The Treasures of Heaven are not Ne-
gations of Passion but Realities of In-
tellect from which All the Passions
Emanate (Uncurbed) in their Eternal
Glory... ["A Vision of the Last
Judgment"]

feats its own purposes and goals. Those goals have everything to do, ideally, with maximizing human happiness and minimizing human misery. Freud's program for social change was primarily sexual. He repeatedly insisted that society should change its standard of sexual morality because it crippled such a significant portion of the population. But he knew that society's conservative bent was sharpest in the area of sexuality, and least likely to change. Thence arose his reluctant conviction that in the one area where man had power to free himself, that of social regulations governing the family, the state, and society, he would keep himself in chains.

Freud held that the source material for art and imagination was ultimately erotic. The structural hypothesis that eventually succeeded the topographical hypothesis in psychoanalytic theory posited libido (sexual energy) as the repository of all unconscious processes. Even the energy for the "work of thought itself must be supplied from sublimated erotic sources."[27] And it is precisely those sources that humans are afraid to acknowledge and will not acknowledge because, according to Freud, their earliest manifestation is incestuous.

Early psychoanalysis might have accomplished its goals more profoundly and efficaciously through subversion. If Freud had called for the early nurture and development of imagination and artistic ability with the force and conviction he used in his pleas for sexual reform, he might have been resisted less—then and now. Again, the seed is present in Freud's own writings. In the essay "'Civilized' Sexual Morality," he remarks that "an abstinent artist is scarcely conceivable.... The production of the artist is probably powerfully stimulated by his sexual experience."[28] This statement has the ring of stereotype, perhaps even of legend, but that does not make it invalid.

Art is the First in Intellectuals & Ought to be First in Nations   [Annotations to the works of Sir Joshua Reynolds]

Enjoyment & not Abstinence is the food of Intellect.   [Blake to George Cumberland, December 6, 1795]

Abstinence sows sand all over
The ruddy limbs & flaming hair
But Desire Gratified Plants fruits of
    life & beauty there
                    ["Songs and Ballads"]

I am reading Freud here as Blake read Milton, and with similar purposes. Blake read Milton as a poet-prophet whose system was more spacious than he knew, and whose mistakes Blake pointed out from his own perspective. According to Blake, Milton made three major mistakes: his muses were those of memory rather than of living imagination; his attitude toward female sexualtiy was wrong-headed; and his dependence on reason limited his capacity for visionary perception. The "Poetic Genius" in him spoke of liberty, sexuality, and energy instead of their pale and inhibited reflections—but not often enough and not strongly enough. Freed of those relatively minor but debilitating "mistakes," Blake's Milton became a giant striding the mountains of Blake's imaginative universe, afire with sexual and intellectual energy.

As I read him, and as he is read by such theorists as Brown and Marcuse, there is a Freud who does not mut-

To bathe in the Waters of Life; to wash off the Not Human
I come in Self-annihilation & the grandeur of Inspiration. . . .
To cast off the rotten rags of Memory by Inspiration. . . .
To cast aside from Poetry, All that is not Inspiration

[*Milton* 41:1–7]

ter, "Anatomy is destiny." He shouts such things as "You can't send people on a Polar expedition with summer clothing and maps of the Italian lakes!" and "Health [is the] unrestricted capacity . . . for production and enjoyment!"[29] And he means it.

This is Freud freed of his mistakes as I perceive them; and, no surprise, his basic "errors" are almost exactly the same as Blake's Milton's. Freud's muses are, literally, those of memory. He was as confused and as confusing in his attitudes toward female sexuality as was Milton, and as wrongheaded. And his dependence on reason made him undervalue the significance of imagination, whose product and process he should have known he was. I enlist the assistance of Blake's poetry to speak for the kind of prophecy Freud said he could not provide. My purpose is twofold. Just as I try to illuminate Freud's strengths and limitations through Blake, I try to suggest a clearer under-

. . . Wandering thro Death's Vale
In conflict with those Female
    Forms. . . .

    [*Milton* 17:6–7]

What is it men in women do require[?]
The lineaments of Gratified Desire[.]
What is it women do in men require[?]
The lineaments of Gratified Desire[.]
        ["Songs and Ballads"]

Now I a fourfold vision see,
And a fourfold vision is given to me;
'Tis fourfold in my supreme delight
And Threefold in soft Beulah's night
And twofold always. May God us keep
From Single vision & Newton's sleep!
[From a poem in a letter to Thomas
Butts, November 22, 1802]

Four Mighty Ones are in every Man.
[*The Four Zoas* 3:4]

Opposition   is   True   Friendship.
[*The Marriage of Heaven and
Hell*, Plate 16]

standing of Blake through Freud.

My contention is that Blake knew everything that Freud knew; that the insights of psychoanalysis were anticipated in large part in Blake's poems and epics. The Blakean annotations here support only a foundation for that contention, of course; they are intended as specific support for the depth of Blake's knowledge of psychic processes. Blake's system was not necessarily greater than Freud's, but it was certainly a more spacious paradigm than Freud's, for it included the "fourth dimension" Blake called Liberty. I do not intend to diminish Freud by comparison. Just as Freud wants Blake to open a closed system, Blake wants Freud in order to be better understood by the twentieth-century mind. Freud's is the first systematic articulation of complete mental activity. I would modify that statement only by saying that his was the first *secular* expression of it, and thus the first to compel

The Eternal Body of Man
is The IMAGINATION
  God himself
that is
  The Divine Body

It manifests itself
in his Works of Art
(In Eternity All is Vision)
    [Inscriptions for "The Laocoön"]

the grudging acknowledg-
ment of Western culture.
  Blake's system was a
visionary allegory of the
same processes. It was mythopoetic, sacred rather
than secular. But as the
dying Gulley Jimson says to
the concerned nun who feels
he should spend his dying
moments praying instead of
laughing: "Same thing,
Mother."[30]

2. They Became What They Beheld

Urizen manacled. From William Blake, *The First Book of Urizen*, Plate 22 (1794). Relief etching. Library of Congress, Rosenwald Collection.

Psychoanalysis began as a system based on contrary tensions, polar oppositions, and dualistic theories of psychic phenomena. It expanded into a system of tripartite structures and triadic theory; yet it always retained its strongly dualistic foundations. Freud posited two basic drives or instincts, the sexual and the aggressive; two basic modes of thought, the primary and the secondary. The early topographical hypothesis was basically twofold: mental activity belonged to the conscious or the unconscious and was correspondingly either manifest or latent. But the introduction of the preconscious as a middle term between the polarities of conscious and unconscious required eventual expansion to a threefold system. Psychoanalysis was free to become essentially tripartite. The "structural hypothesis" posits three interrelated functions, designated conceptually as id, ego, and superego. Three phases are identified in the development of personality: oral, anal, and genital. The family romance is essentially triangular, consisting of mother, father, and child. Normal development is divided into three stages, from birth to the oedipal phase, from the oedipal phase to puberty, from puberty on. Expansions into fourfold formulations are always possible, but Freud seemed wary of them. He did not, for instance, pursue the transformations between puberty and "maturity," as he might have.

Psychoanalysis retained one obvious advantage of a threefold system, a kind of irreducibility. It is more difficult to remember and to conceptualize in fours, as Blake's system demands. For Blake, the resistance of the mind to fourfold vision, or at least its inherent disposition to reduce it, is the condition of "Fall." In the "natural world," subject to the largely self-imposed restrictions

75

of time and space, the fourfold vision is always in danger of reduction to the twofold: the mind thinks in terms of subject and object. The most reduced form of the fourfold is "single Vision," which is solipsistic, self-absorbed, totally nonproductive. The least degree of reduction is the threefold vision, which requires an expansion beyond the dualistic in conceptual terms. Three is the number Blake attributed to sexuality in its expansive form.

The fourth dimension of imaginative liberty is a redemptive overlay on other ways of thinking, interacting, and being in the world. From the imaginative perspective, positive as well as negative valuations are possible for the first three modes of relating. Oneness need not signify brooding subjectivity, but can mean wholeness and unity. Twofold vision is the source of subject–object schisms, but can also be "holy Generation Image of Regeneration" (*Jerusalem* 1:7:65). Three can be the self-sufficient triad that collapses into negative oneness when divided by itself, but it can also be the pivotal phase of relating for imaginative transformation.

The correspondences between Blake's and Freud's systems are within the onefold, twofold, and especially the threefold structures. They differ in their idea of prime causation, and the fourth dimension operates actively only in Blake's system. Freud starts from a biologically, historically determined and deterministic model, the birth of the individual and of civilization. Blake starts from an imaginatively determined and nondeterministic model. For Blake, the birth of the individual and of culture is "preceded" by an eternity in which form and matter are identical. He expressed the characteristics of eternity in terms of energy: fluid, flowing, imaginative, intellectual, a spirit world not shadowy and insubstantial, but clear, precise, and real, that is, bodied.

To account for the separation of form and matter, Blake posited a primal cleavage, the act called creation. Creation is fall for Blake because it sunders form and matter, yielding the natural world ruled by time and space, into which human beings come as mortal, biological, discrete entities. Freud demonstrated the mental nature of the deepest layers of human existence, which flows from a source of energy whose scope and movement become hidden in the normal process of individual and cultural development. Deep in each person's past, and in humankind's phylogenetic past, is a more resonant psychic past. Blake posits this deep, remote mental past (rather than the remote biological past) as the ground of being, the source from which matter itself generates.

Limitation of the ability to speak of this past is inherent in language, itself a creation of the cleavage and a product of being-in-nature. We are stuck with the images we know, but Blake presses them to our service in the attempt to imagine what might have preceded them. As I read it, his argument comes to this: If people imagine grounds of being that minimize the value of being human, then humankind will fall to the task of recovery, and not rise to it. Blake emphasizes sources of strength and freedom in the attempt to transcend natural restriction, and those sources are always ultimately mental. Mental causation is deeper than sexual causation. "The Treasures of Heaven are not Negations of Passion but Realities of Intellect from which all the passions Emanate Uncurbed."[1] If people imagine small and wish small, they will only reproduce their external restrictions.

Similarly, if people define immortality as a continuation of individual bodily consciousness—that is, things as they are, writ large and enduring perpetually—then they imagine very little. They especially reduce themselves if they imagine a God greater and higher than they, who hands out reward and punishment like a father in a family. The traditional concept of heaven is merely a reproduction of familial relationships. The whole idea is not original, or rehabilitating, or even very appealing, thinks Blake, except to those instincts that are conservative, repetitive, and fearful. It is little better to declare God dead, and replace him with a sense of natural destiny or fate.

"The desire of Man being Infinite the possession is Infinite & himself Infinite."[2] If mental life is the deepest and potentially freest aspect of humanity, let us imagine that in the beginning was mental energy, animating everything. Let us call that energy human, and restore ourselves to mythic stature. There is no way to "know" what form that energy took when form and energy were undivided. But if what is left of that mental/imaginative/intellectual energy is now housed in a body, why not poetically, mythically, imagine an unfallen and expansive body that corresponds to our own? The human form divine becomes an expansion of what we now have. Transcendence, in this paradigm, is connected to, rather than isolated from, the present and the body. The fallen mind and body should not be despised because people are not so free or so perfect as they might wish. Blake's ideal differs sharply from ideals that perpetuate dualities of body and mind. We should, he says, love body and mind for their mythic potential, and actively seek to realize that potential. In short, sex and art, loving and imagining, are the ways Blake says people can imagine and act out whatever they posit as eternal values.

Human beings imagine themselves as mind trapped in body, and that perspective keeps them ever divided against themselves, and makes freedom a manifest impossibility. Heaven and hell are states of mind and body within, but people project both outside themselves. Heaven, freedom, and happiness are either relinquished or relegated to "an allegorical abode where existence hath never come."[3] Hell is the renunciation of freedom and the denial of imagination, by which we accomplish the punishment we fear. It is not up to the gods to mend this mess, says Blake. All deities reside in the human breast, and all demons as well.

Whether or not this ideal mythic past ever really existed is absolutely irrelevant to the workings of Blake's system. The very need to fix historical accuracy is to test imagination against the alien standard of matter, to trap timelessness in time and infinity in space. That need consumes human beings in questions of what was and will be at the perpetual expense of what is and can be in the present moment.

Freud saw the development of matter and mind to its present

form in the individual and culture as fundamentally progressive, albeit with regressive trends that occupied the greater part of his clinical and theoretical attention. Blake saw the same development as fundamentally regressive, albeit with the potential for progression through regeneration of the ideal from which he began. They meet where Freud begins, with birth, creation, and biological evolution in the natural world. And in this natural world, Blake sees as clearly as Freud the sexual causation of all thought and event. Freud classed the intellectual processes among displacements of sexual energy. "The energy for the work of thought itself must be supplied from sublimated erotic sources."[4] From the visionary or fourth-fold perspective, the formulation must be reversed. But from the natural perspective, Blake would agree that Freud's formulation is exactly correct.

Freud's reasons for finding individual and cultural development basically progressive are the products of his restricted ideal—an ideal he would call realistic. The compromises with instinctual gratification that are for Freud definitive of health form a fair copy of Blake's definition of sickness. Freud says that the purpose of life is to pursue the pleasure principle, "and yet its programme is at loggerheads with the whole world, with the macrocosm as well as the microcosm. There is no possibility at all of its being carried through; all the regulations of the universe run counter to it."[5] Since Freud's macrocosm is the natural world, his conclusion is absolutely determined and impeccably correct. In the late essay "Analysis Terminable and Interminable," Freud defined the desirable outcome of the therapeutic process as "the liberation of a human being from his neurotic symptoms, inhibitions, and abnormalities of character."[6] A fundamental paradox of Freudian methodology is neatly summarized here. One cannot be simultaneously liberated from inhibitions and abnormalities of character when inhibitions are definitive of normality. It is a contradiction in Freud's own terms. If the ends of therapy are to conform to a norm that is itself the product of excessive repression, then freedom from inhibitions is not a consonant means to that end. Freud concedes, later in the same essay, that the "normal ego" is itself an "ideal fiction"—it is, in other words, anything but normal.

Freud's program for change through "realistic" compromise between opposing trends within the individual and between the individual and culture is essentially cautious and conservative. Blake, on the other hand, thought that even the sensible compromises that ought to be possible seldom work out well, that they are also an "ideal fiction." Even if they could work, Blake would find them of little use. Adjustment to external reality and capitulation to natural limitation (activities that Freud himself perceived consume the majority of man's time and energy with no guarantee and often no good result) were for Blake a waste of time.

Freud credited repression of libido with sole responsibility for cultural and individual misery. He knew it was impossible for a person to be healthy if the maintenance of repression took all of his available energy. It was for this reason that he was labeled a hedonist. He protested this accusation as unfair and inaccurate. The fact that he recognized the power of the pleasure principle and the price paid for its repression did not mean, he continually asserted, that he advocated full and immediate gratification of impulse. Pleasure was of itself amoral, and Freud was a moralist who appeared to his contemporaries to be a hedonist. Blake was an antimoralist who advocated the active pursuit of "the lineaments of gratified desire."

In the emerging climate of what would later be called romanticism, Blake was freer than Freud to define gratification of desire in hopeful and expansive ways. For Freud, unconscious impulse was the tyrant of conscious life; repressed material must be brought to consciousness if people were to get through life with minimal pain and maximal pleasure. For Blake, unconscious impulse was also the tyrant of conscious life. His program, like Freud's, was for disclosure of the hidden, but with this definitive difference: in Blake's system, the division and contraction of the unconscious generates consciousness, which is rational and thus limited. The conscious and the rational become in turn the real tyrants that circumscribe man's possibilities. For Freud, the transformation from unconscious to conscious at its best takes some of the same forms it does for Blake—art and love— but for Freud, the conversion is from an essentially negative original state to a morally positive one, through the process of sublimation. "And thus it is that what belongs to the lowest depths in the mind of each one of us is changed . . . into what we value as the highest in the human soul."[7] For Blake, the conversion more often works in the opposite direction. Unconscious energy, "Eternal delight," is harnessed by rational consciousness and converted into restriction, pain, and repression. Blake was aware of the potential voraciousness of untempered aggressive impulse, as evidenced by the "Spectre" in each "Humanity." But that spectre is a product of repressed libido as well, and takes on its evil character through and after the conversion to consciousness, not before it, as with Freud.

Both systems include aggressive and libidinal drives, but the drives are differently determined. Freud distrusted libido as much as he distrusted aggressive/destructive instinct. Any positive, humanistic action was by definition the product of sublimation conversion. Freud's differentiation of sexual and aggressive does not translate into "good" and "evil" merely because one tends toward pleasure and life, the other toward pain and death. He thought himself above those moral categories. But even the most superficial reading of Freud yields the impression that both were often "evil" categories for Freud. If the id impulses are all amoral, as Freud thought, his own moralist stance automatically converted "amoral" into "immoral."

Blake posited the repository of the unconscious as innately full of potential. The appellation of good and evil, or of any moral categories at all, was in Blake's view the result of the fall. Blake, like Freud at his freest, saw the possibility and the grave need for a kind of transformation other than that from amoral to moral or immoral. In order to speak of it at all, he was compelled to use those categories he despised. He reversed their traditional content in *The Marriage of Heaven and Hell*. "Good is the passive that obeys Reason. Evil is the active springing from Energy" (Plate 3). He made it perfectly clear which he thought was really positive and which negative. Man could and must reverse the determinism that arises from positing energy, action, and pleasure as fundamentally evil.

Man seldom rose above that determinism, and Blake prophesied what would happen if he did not, what had happened because he did not, and what could happen only if he did. Sex could be associated with pleasure and love, but only if what passed for love in the fallen world were clearly recognized. Man could become his own master, but only if he perceived the tyrannies under which he lived, so that he might overthrow them. What Freud called the disclosure of latent content or repressed material is what Blake meant by the necessity to "give a body to Error," so that it might be cast out. Man could see with more than the eye, but only when he knew that the eye, the category of the perceived, had dominated his personal and his species' history.

Blake insisted that the category of the perceived—the seen and therefore known—was only one aspect of existence. For Freud, it seemed to be the all. Freud's observation model was often exactly that: one in which the "observed" was the totality of the existing.[8] And yet it is at this very point that distinctions between Blake and Freud yield to profounder similarities. Freud was rejected by empiricists on the ground that his "proofs" were not proofs at all. They were all indirect. Psychoanalysis rests its case on the unknown and unseen, or rather the indirectly known and seen. Disconnected and unintelligible conscious acts will fall into demonstrable connection only "if we interpolate the unconscious acts that we infer."[9]

Interpolation and inference are the means of Freudian "proof." Freud's observation model was almost entirely anagogic and inferential, so that according to traditional empirical categories, he was antiempirical and antirational. He claimed that the seen and known are only special cases or derivatives of what can be seen and known. It is perhaps this perception, more than any other, that directs my comparison of Blake and Freud. Freud attempted to revolutionize the nature of proof and of experience-based data. This expansion of perception in Freud meets the expansion of perception in Blake. For each in his own way, the rational faculty is itself the faulty and limited perceptual category. The reality of the unseen is their common ground. The scope and nature of the unseen is the ground of their difference.

The central tenets of Freud's psychoanalysis are contained in cryptic form in *The Songs of Innocence and Experience, The Book of Thel, The Marriage of Heaven and Hell, Visions of the Daughters of Albion*, and the other "minor prophecies" known as the Lambeth Books. Elaborations, revisions, and refinements of psychoanalytic theory are contained in the later "major prophecies," just as Freud's are found in theoretical texts in and after 1921 with the publication of *Beyond the Pleasure Principle* and *The Ego and the Id*.

The dual theory of drives and the structural hypothesis are now regarded as pivotal points in the subsequent development of psychoanalytic theory. Thereafter, Freud was obliged not only to expand but to backread that expansion into all that came before. Blake's system underwent a parallel development on one level. His early perspectives are styled as confrontations between contraries: innocence and experience, heaven and hell, good and evil, masculine and feminine. In terms of his later diction, the early works concentrate on the activities proper to single and twofold vision: on Ulro and Generation. The polar tensions of the early Blakean universe are very like Freud's early dualistic stylizations of unconscious and conscious, pleasure principle and reality principle, primary and secondary process.

Neither Freud nor Blake completely abandoned early formulations. Rather, they were accommodated to later developments and revised accordingly. It is as true of men's philosophical systems as of their psychic constitutions that early foundations are never torn down, but exist side by side with later constructions. For Freud, the final product was always contained in embryo in its beginnings, whether the subject was the vicissitudes of a character trait, the first and final drafts of a poem, or the foundation and fall of empire. Transformations in psychoanalytic theory are advances, but it is to be expected that Freud's tripartite conception of psyche was latent in the structure of the topographical hypothesis. Blake's major developments can be characterized in several ways. The contraries, essentially two-dimensional, did not remain sufficient metaphors for the development of Blake's system. The later works explore the nature of the threefold, which Blake called the sexual, and the fourfold, or human. Just as the triadic structure was prefigured in early Freud, the third and fourth dimensions were present in Blake's early work.

The primary difference in the somewhat analogous development of the two systems is, I think, that the third dimension is manifest in Blake's early theories, while it remains latent in Freud's. Similarly, Blake's system was dual from its inception with respect to developments that were originally monistic in Freud's early works, and became dualistic only later in his career. The theory of dual drives—libidinal and aggressive/conservative—is a relatively late postulate in Freud. In *Beyond the Pleasure Principle*, Freud summarized the inborn conservatism of biological tendencies: "The aim of all life is death." The destructive drives represent "the inertia inherent in organic life" and "the conservative nature of all living substance."[10] As the product of being-in-nature, Freud thought these destructive components inescapable, literally because men die and psychically because the "compulsion to repeat" exercises a powerful retarding influence over life activity. As "a piece of unconquerable nature" in psychic constitution, it accounts for the puzzling "resistance to the discovery of resistances" which "defends itself by all possible means against recovery."[11]

Freud's reluctance to present this controversial thesis in 1920 was more than merely rhetorical. Since his was a system in which the "natural" was both the valley and the summit of human possibility, he was dismayed to find it so recalcitrant an ally. Man was man's natural enemy, not just his conditioned enemy. This discovery partially accounts for the relatively late appearance of the dual drive theory in psychoanalysis, and also for its inevitable postulation. As a natural scientist, Freud based mental causation, or psychic determinism, on extended analogy with natural causation. The analogy was more than metaphorical. What Freud tried to demonstrate was that psychic determinism is itself a category of natural determinism; no less, and decidedly no more.

Blake shared this conviction about biological destiny. In the later works, he expressed the situation as succinctly as is possible, calling this "a world in which man is by his nature the enemy of man" (*Jerusalem* 43:52). But the theory of "dual drives," sexual and aggressive, life-directed and death-oriented, was already present in the writings of the 1790s. What Freud came to reluctantly and late, Blake thought axiomatic. Being-in-nature is by definition a "fallen state" for Blake.[12] Urizen's fall in the 1794 *Book of Urizen* is imaged as a fall into bodily limitation in the natural world.

> 6. And Urizen craving with hunger
> Stung with the odours of Nature
> Explor'd his dens around.

Since, in Blake's view, nature is not the summit of possibility that it is for Freud, he could acknowledge its limitations at the outset. It is true that while the later prophecies develop the redemptive potential of the fourth fold, they also increase in vehemence against the natural. More and more of Blake's energy became occupied with the necessity to do battle with necessity if imaginative life were to be realized within the constraints of the natural. In that respect, developments in the two systems are analogous, for Freud was also increasingly engaged in bemoaning natural limitation. However, Blake's early perception of both negative and positive valuations of the threefold make it possible, and even necessary, to compare early Blake with late Freud. The outlines of tripartite psychic development in id, ego, and superego are present in *The Songs of Experience, The Book of Thel*, and *Visions of the Daughters of Albion*, all works of the late 1780s to mid-1790s.

3. Innocence and Experience

Los, Orc, and Enitharmon. From William Blake, *The First Book of Urizen,* Plate 21 (1794). Relief etching. Library of Congress, Rosenwald Collection.

Innocence:
The Book of Thel

A baby is born. Freud called that event "the prototype of all later danger situations which arose under the new conditions imposed by an altered form of existence, and by the advance of psychic development." Freud never agreed with Otto Rank about an *actual* determination of the birth trauma as the foundation of neurosis. Rather, he specified that "its own significance is limited to this prototype relationship to danger."[1] In other words, Freud employed the birth trauma as a metaphor. And what he metaphorically called the prototypical trauma of birth, Blake metaphorically called creation and fall.

> My mother groand! my father wept.
> Into the dangerous world I leapt:
> Helpless, naked, piping loud;
> Like a fiend hid in a cloud.
> ["Infant Sorrow," *Songs of Experience*]

Freud's prelude to the "altered form of existence" is intrauterine life. For Blake, the prelude is something before, beyond, and transcending intrauterine life. For both, the newborn evokes potential feelings of terror and beauty. Neither harbored completely unalloyed feelings of tenderness toward the infant. Babies often drive Freud to exclamation points. "So great is the greed of the childish libido!" The "love" of the baby "knows no bounds, demands exclusive possession, is satisfied with nothing less than all."[2] For Blake, who celebrated "infant joy," "infant sorrow" could also be terrible.

89

> Struggling in my father's hands:
> Striving against my swadling bands:
> Bound and weary I thought best
> To sulk upon my mother's breast.

In *The Book of Urizen*, the first infant birth (as distinct from the birth of the sexes) is an event looked on by the eternals with terror. "A shriek ran through Eternity / And a paralytic stroke." The child Orc is born howling, and issues from his mother's womb with "fierce flames." The development of the fetus in the mother's womb is imaged in almost Darwinian evolutionary stages: from worm to "many forms of fish, bird & beast." The response of the eternals is uncompromising. They close their tent and "beat down the stakes." They are responding in part to the spectacle of man begetting his image on his divided self, and to the terrible form the issue takes.

Freud called the "fierce flames" of the newborn infant "libido." In later formulations, we have seen that he concluded that the child is born with innate aggressive/destructive instincts as well. Freud is prone to dour pronouncements on the "stubbornness" and "insubordination" of the infant's libido, which must be brought under control. But for Blake, the danger is in the deflection of impulse rather than its indulgence. The infant's energy is eternal delight. His destructive/aggressive impulses are not what Blake terms energy; they are the antithesis of true energy, and their manifestation is the perversion of energy. (The significant partial exception to this rule is that aggressive energy is often needed in order to counter oppression and repression. That is a special case, which I shall examine later.) The newborn of "Infant Sorrow" is a "fiend" only because his parents restrain his energy in swaddling bands, so that he is "hid in a cloud." His struggling and striving are not negative. Rather, his inability to break free is the inhibiting and destructive event. It is because he is "bound" that he sulks upon his mother's breast. All the potential energy of infancy is driven into the mirror relationship of mother and infant in the nursing situation. What appears to Freud as "greed" appears the same to Blake, but for different reasons. Greed is forced upon the infant, according to Freud, because of "the protracted helplessness of human infancy." Freud might call it the human condition, but Blake would call it the less-than-human condition.

Blake's infant is naturally and radically both innocent and libidinal. It is civilization that labels libidinal innocence as corruption.

> Infancy, fearless, lustful, happy! nestling for delight
> In laps of pleasure; Innocence! honest, open, seeking
> The vigorous joys of morning light; open to virgin bliss. . . .
> [*Visions of the Daughters of Albion*]

For Freud, health consists in mastery over both the libidinal and destructive instincts, by which means he hopes that people may attain "the unrestricted capacity for enjoyment."[3] For Blake, the tragedy of human life is inherent in the mastery of libidinal instinct. The nurturing of destructive instinct, rather than its transformation, seems to him to be the major accomplishment of civilization.

In *Songs of Innocence*, the familial situation is loving and supportive. Parental imagos are permitters rather than restrainers. There mercy, pity, peace, and love are "virtues of delight," and the nurse does not require the children to come in while "it is yet day." Infant joy is "sweet," children laugh and play, the green is very green indeed, nature is always friendly, glowworms show the way home, lions weep tears of tenderness. When biological fathers are not near, God, "like his father in white," magically appears. Yet this is not a world devoid of sorrow. Children and emmets are lost in the dark before God or glowworms appear, the robin sobs while the sparrow is merry, the chimney sweep's mother is dead and his father has sold him, and Jesus must "sit by us and moan" in order "that our grief he may destroy." If it took readers many years to see these things in *Songs of Innocence*, it is because they, like the inhabitants of the songs, have already undergone the process of repression. The children of innocence do not think of sex, but they fear the dark. Their parents watch

them play and remember, "Such were the joys / When we all girls
& boys." Children and parents alike in the *Songs* know little of
the sources of their fears or their joys. That their author did in
1789 might not be adequately demonstrable in the *Songs* themselves, but is clear in *The Book of Thel*, dated the same year.

> O life of this our spring! why fades the lotus of the water?
> Why fade these children of the spring? born but to smile &
>   fall.
> Ah! Thel is like a watry bow, and like a parting cloud,
> Like a reflection in a glass. like shadows in the water.
> Like dreams of infants. like a smile upon an infants face,
> Like the doves voice, like transient day, like music in the air;
>   [*The Book of Thel*, Plate 1, 6–11]

The "virgin of the skies" and "queen of the Vales of Har" is a
natural innocent. In the commonplace critical formulation for
The Book of Thel, she represents innocence rejecting experience.
Her home in the Vales of Har represents the overripeness and
eventual decay of the state of fearful innocence. The children of
The Songs of Innocence inhabit a world much like hers, but their
conflicts are latent. They fear the dark and they fear getting lost,
but they do not know why. Thel is no longer a child. Her conflicts are those of awakening puberty, and her moment is the
time in which the latent becomes manifest. The manifest subject
of Thel's laments is her mortality. She mourns her transience,
and sees herself as a natural creature in analogy with the lotus
and the dove, the rainbow and the cloud. The "glass" is what
Blake later names the "vegetable glass of nature" or "Enitharmon's looking glass." Thel's perspective is both natural and
naive. In Freudian terms, reluctance to accept the fate of
mortality is a product of the narcissistic phase, during which the
individual is her own ideal.[4]

In answer to her laments, the lily and the cloud tell Thel that
"every thing that lives, / Lives not alone, nor for itself" (Plate 3).
They encourage her to accept her place in the chain of nature.
God loves even the worm, and he has married the earth, whom

he calls "mother of my children." Though she will be "the food of worms," the earth is life as well as death, womb as well as tomb. Thel is comforted by this assurance, for she takes it to mean that her being-in-nature will end in a comforting, asexual union with Father God and Mother Earth. There is no mention of sexuality. For Thel, mortality is the only conscious issue. The earth invites her to "enter my house" and explore the caverns of the grave. She wandered

> Till to her own grave plot she came, & there she sat down.
> And heard this voice of sorrow breathed from the hollow pit.
>
> Why cannot the Ear be closed to its own destruction?
> Or the glistning Eye to the poison of a smile!
> Why are Eyelids stord with arrows ready drawn,
> Where a thousand fighting men in ambush lie?
> Or an Eye of gifts & graces, show'ring fruits & coined gold!
> Why a Tongue impress'd with honey from every wind?
> Why an Ear, a whirlpool fierce to draw creations in?
> Why a Nostril wide inhaling terror trembling & affright
> Why a tender curb upon the youthful burning boy!
> Why a little curtain of flesh on the bed of our desire?
>
> The virgin started from her seat, & with a shriek.
> Fled back unhinderd till she came into the vales of Har.
>
> [*The Book of Thel*, Plate 6]

The unidentified voice from Thel's grave is her own, an unconscious voice literally as well as figuratively buried. Until this moment of confrontation with her own eventual death, Thel has successfully repressed the roots of her mortal fear. The caverns of the grave are the deepest reaches of the unconscious, and "the secrets of the land unknown" are wishes and fears. The topography of *The Book of Thel* is symbolic psychic topography; aboveground are consciousness and manifest content, and beneath the earth are unconsciousness and latent content. When the clay invites Thel to enter ("'tis given thee to enter, / And to return") she is inviting Thel to explore her own internal recesses without the protective veil that blocks direct perception in normal states of mind. The "fibrous roots of every heart" in the land of the dead are not only mortal remains, but psychic sources of what appears on the surface of earth and mind. (A cautionary note for this uncluttered formula: for Blake, unconsciousness and instinctual impulse are not categories that exist only below consciousness, but above and beyond consciousness as well. The portion that exists beyond consciousness is, however, the visionary perspective of the fourth fold. In the "natural" perspective of *The Book of Thel*, the fourth fold is present only by inference, so that unconsciousness, or primary process, is limited to depth.)

"The return of the repressed" for Thel is not a slow process resulting in symptom formation, but rather an instant, naked confrontation. It is not only, or even primarily, death she fears. She sits and listens to the voice through the catalogue of sensual limitation and duplicity in ear, eye, tongue, and nostril. What sends her screaming back to the Vales of Har is the prospect of the "youthful burning boy" bursting the "little curtain of flesh." Why should sexual instinct so frighten her? What in her own sexual disposition could work against her? Freud's answer to that problem in the individual is this:

> The individual does actually carry on a double existence: one designed to serve his own purposes and another as a link in a chain, in which he serves against, or at any rate without, any volition of his own. The individual himself regards sexuality as one of his own aims; while from another point of view, he is only an appendage to his germ-plasm, to which he lends his energies, taking in return his toll of pleasure. . . . The differentiation of the sexual instincts from the ego instincts would simply reflect this double function of the individual.[5]

In this relatively early formulation (1914), the pressure toward mortality has its source in external pressure exerted on the ego by nature and in internal pressure exerted on the ego by the unwitting cooperation of the sexual instincts. To the extent that libidinal object cathexes are "egosyntonic," they are not in conflict with the individual's narcissistic ideal. Sexual energy can be directed toward an object without depleting the ego, and the result is genuine reciprocity between ego libido and object libido. But repressed libido produces a deflection from the sexual aim so that love is experienced as depletion and the "re-enrichment of the ego can be effected only by a withdrawal of libido from its objects."[6]

Thel's early laments reflect her crisis of the "double existence." She lives for herself, but then she fades away without trace. She superficially reconciles herself to the double existence on the strength of the comforting promise that she will endure as part of a transcendent familial situation. At the moment of entering the grave, Thel is at the very point of embracing mortality through sexuality, poised on the brink of transferring libido from self to object. But Thel has a past. She is not an infant, but a young woman who has never been faced with the task of relinquishing her love, and thereby part of her self, to another. Trapped in perpetual innocence with her mother and sisters in the Vales of Har, she has been her own ego ideal. Freud called the formation of that ideal "the most powerful factor favoring repression."[7] That her personality development has undergone this process of repression is evident in her mistaken understanding of what she fears and why.

But the psychic situation of *The Book of Thel* cannot be adequately explained by reference to Freud's early formulations on narcissism, because those early theories posit only that fear of death *contributes to* the fear of sex, and vice versa. In *The Book of Thel*, fear of mortality is ultimately revealed as a cover for fear of sexuality—not that death is not itself a real fear, but in Thel's case, the deeper and causative factor is sexuality. Again Blake anticipates Freud. In and after *Beyond the Pleasure Principle,* the internal component of the connection between death and sexuality is developed in such a way that the obligation of the sexual instinct to serve the natural chain is reinforced by the (self-) destructive instincts as well. For Blake, it is literally in the nature of the senses to exert pressure toward death as well as life, reduction as well as expansion. In psychoanalytic terminology, the theory of dual drives, sexual and destructive, is contained in the lament from the grave. After 1920, Freud maintained that death fear in civilized man is attributable in large part to pre-oedipal and oedipal conflict. The castration complex in both sexes *is* the death complex, the anticipated punishment for sexual/ aggressive desires in the family romance. The fear of death is also the end of a sequence of separation anxieties that may be traced to the earliest separation from the mother and the mother's breast.[8]

Blake conflates all of these elements in the lament from the grave. Identification of the speaker might seem the least of the problems presented by this passage. It is a series of questions without answers; the text both gives and withholds. At one moment, the voice seems to be lamenting the restrictions of the senses, and at the next—or even the same—to rue their expansiveness. The tone is simultaneously assertive, sad, helpless, angry, and fierce. For every question, there might be two or more answers that seem to be mutually exclusive. "Why cannot the ear be closed to its own destruction?" it begins. One unwritten answer: The body is mortal, and it knows of its own mortality from the inside. The ear is a realist. It hears the sounds of pain as well as those of joy. Another answer: If the ear were closed to its own destruction, it would be deaf as well to its salvation, which has the same sources. A third: The ear should and can be closed to its own destruction. The answer depends on the perspective of the reader or the hearer.

The hearer in the text is Thel. If the voice is that of her own unconsciousness, the ambiguity of the passage becomes not a problem but an inevitability. The distinction between wish and fear disappears. As an articulation of internal conflict, the voice must ask questions that admit of paradoxical responses, unresolved and irresolvable in logical terms. The passage is usually read as an indictment of sensual limitation, and from one perspective, it is exactly that. But from another perspective, it is also a defense against the expansive potential of the senses. Or to be more precise, among the potential "answers" are defenses against potential expansion. (The process of defense is an ego process; thus it is Thel's consciousness, her ego, that must choose a response to questions that have no single answer in the unconscious.)

The eye is open to "the poison of a smile," the smile of the other, the love object toward whom libido may be directed. The eye is also "stord with arrows ready drawn, / Where a thousand fighting men in ambush lie." It is therefore open to love, which from the narcissistic stance is always potentially dangerous. The eye defends against love with drawn arrows and fighting men, yet those same arrows can be the arrows of desire, ready to "attack" as well as to defend. The ear "draws creations in," that is, reduces by capturing, but contains those worlds it can expand by "hearing" more. Thel is hearing her own paradoxical wishes and fears to be closed and open to self and beloved others. The senses are all lines of demarcation, bodily boundaries between self and other, or internal and external, which must be traversed if one is to love. The danger in remaining self-contained is that refusal to risk destruction is simultaneously rejection of the means to escape destruction.

The final and decisive boundary for Thel is the hymen, the "little curtain of flesh." It is her most precious boundary, the point of conflict between ego libido and object libido. Its invasion by the youthful burning boy on the bed of their mutual desire signifies complete loss of self to Thel, the dissolution of ego boundaries that is experienced in love. That "boundarilessness" is the very essence of eroticism, which Georges Bataille calls "assenting to life to the point of death."[9] Thel is unable to face her own aggressive sexual desire, as well as the boy's. She chooses instead to withdraw libido into herself, in order to protect those ego boundaries. "The body itself," Freud wrote in 1923, "is a place from which both internal and external perceptions may spring.... The ego is first and foremost a body-ego."[10]

Thel fears the duplicitousness of sexuality in every respect. The "poison of a smile" may signify false love. But even genuine love participates in the natural/mortal as well as the imaginative/immortal. Thel represents, on one level, a genderless "failure" to embrace experience. But the world of experience and generation in Blake is a world of sexuality. By refusing to enter it, Thel also functions as Freud's narcissistic woman, who wants to be loved but cannot love in return.[11] Thel looks at what is offered and decides, in the words of a southern American aphorism, that it's too much sugar for a dime.

Experience: The Family Romance

Songs of Experience present one perspective on the world of generation that Thel refused. Reading them, one is easily convinced that Thel's refusal was not, after all, injudicious. The familial situation, loving and nurturing in the *Songs of Innocence*, is restrictive and repressive in the *Songs of Experience*. Parental figures in the form of priest, father, nurse, and mother become the restrainers of youthful sexuality and individuation. The "father of ancient men," Freud's primal-horde father and his followers, is the "selfish father of men / Cruel jealous selfish fear" that binds free love in "this heavy chain" ("Earth's Answer"). The nurse projects her sexual frustration and fear onto the children whom she charges to come home, for "your spring and your day are wasted in play / And your winter and night in disguise" ("Nurse's Song").

"Detaching himself from his family becomes a task that faces every young person," Freud wrote.[12] "To Tirzah" is Blake's poetic expression of that tenet, expressed in almost brutal terms.

> Thou Mother of my Mortal part
> With cruelty didst mould my Heart,
> And with false self-decieving tears,
> Didst bind my Nostrils Eyes & Ears.
>
> Didst close my Tongue in senseless clay
> And me to mortal life betray:

The Death of Jesus set me free,
Then what have I to do with thee?

In Blake's mythology, Tirzah is natural necessity, and the persona's rejection is on one level a turning away from bodily limitation. But the poem operates on the personal and literally familial level as well. Its biblical allusion is to Christ's curious rejection of Mary, which Blake read as a refusal to be tied to mortality. The analogue in every individual's life is the necessity to break free of the mother–child bond in order to achieve individual freedom, the liberty to go and grow one's own way. Yet the tone seems harsh for that context. Is it really necessary to damn one's mother in order to grow up? Is parental love really "cruel" and "self-decieving"? Both Blake and Freud say yes. "Parental love, which is so touching and at bottom so childish, is nothing but parental narcissism born again and, transformed though it be into object-love, it reveals its former character infallibly."[13]

The parent is not, of course, aware of this derivation. That lack of awareness makes the result the more insidious. The sex of the speaker in the poem is not specified; it might be either male or female, for each sex must reject the mother for its own psychic reasons. The bond with the mother is the earliest and in some ways the strongest of all bonds. It is broken only by violent means, whether that violence is internal or external. For the female, resolution of the "castration complex" in Freud's terms means a turning away from the mother, who "has not given her a proper genital." In other words, part of "normal" female development in our society is resentment at being born a woman. The original mother object must be exchanged for the father— and the father for someone else. Blake's poem fits the first stage of the Freudian formulation very well in the girl's instance, for the speaker's tone is openly reproachful for the "betrayal" to "mortal life"—powerless, penisless life, in psychoanalytic terms.

The vehement rejection of the mother is just as serious an issue for the boy, for different reasons. For him, according to Freud, it is perceived literally as a matter of life and death. The castration complex begins the resolution of the oedipal complex in the male. The boy fears castration by his father for nursing sexual desire toward his mother and aggressive feelings toward his father as competitor. He must turn away from his mother, identify with his father, and turn toward love objects other than his mother. The residue of the castration complex in the boy is a "measure of disparagement in his attitude toward women."[14] That disparagement is one possible reading of the tone of "To Tirzah" when the speaker is read as a male. I say one possible reading because the "visionary" perspective on this poem would require a very different reading of the meaning of mother rejection and the desirable outcome of that rejection. But in fact the outcome Freud regards as normal and desirable is the one Blake knew most often resulted, whether desirable or not. That is, the rejection of the mother, which should open onto a visionary perspective, tends instead to result in hatred and disparagement of women. These are, after all, songs of experience.

The object love of parents, which is "so touching" but at bottom so selfish, is characteristic of all object love, in Freud's view. Blake's perception is articulated in "The Clod and the Pebble":

> Love seeketh not Itself to please,
> Nor for itself hath any care;
> But for another gives it ease,
> And builds a Heaven in Hell's despair.

That is one way, says Blake, to perceive love. It is the best and tenderest way, but not the most realistic in the world of experience, where nothing is as it seems on the surface.

> Love seeketh only Self to please,
> To bind another to its delight;
> Joys in anothers loss of ease,
> And builds a Hell in Heavens despite.

The first speaker is the clod of clay, "trodden with cattles feet." It is giving and resilient, and it lives on the surface of the earth, which is again the conscious level of perception. The second speaker is the pebble, hard and cold, and its place is underneath the surface of the water, which I read as signifying the latent content of love. The clod is an innocent, the pebble is not. The clod's portion of the poem is thematically a song of innocence, the pebble's a song of experience. Critics are fond of pairing poems from *Innocence* and *Experience* and presenting them as contraries. I read them here with the same topographical model I used for reading *The Book of Thel*. That reading is compatible with Blake's insistence that his poems be read as a drama continually enacted in every human heart. The paired poems of innocence and experience then become part of the pattern of psychic contraries in conscious and unconscious, manifest and latent levels of interpretation. A case in point that continues the discussion above is "The Divine Image" (from *Innocence*) and "The Human Abstract" (from *Experience*). In "The Divine Image," mercy, pity, peace, and love are "virtues of delight" that possess the human heart, face, form, and dress. But in "The Human Abstract," pity is the result of making somebody poor, "And Mercy no more could be, / If all were as happy as we."

> And mutual fear brings peace;
> Till the selfish loves increase.

Freud's voice again a hundred years later: "What belongs to the lowest depths in the minds of each one of us is changed . . . into what we value as the highest in the human soul."[15] This is the very essence of sublimation and the cornerstone of civilization. Blake saw its hidden content as clearly as Freud. The imaginative perspective can always redeem reality, but when not redeemed, Blake's vision of reality as most people experience it was fully as black as Freud's. The two "Holy Thursdays" are another accessible example of manifest tenderness yielding latent brutality, for the "aged men wise guardians of the poor" are revealed as "the cold and usurous hand."

And what of the father? The father figures in *Songs of Experience* are closely connected with priests, organized religion, and the formation of the superego. These connections are implicit in

"The Garden of Love," where "Thou shalt not" is writ over the door. The pairing of father and priest is Blake's early analogy of cultural and individual development. The analogy matches Freud's in the minutest details. In Freudian theory, normal libidinal development is accomplished by repression and sublimation of instinct. "The liberty of the individual is no gift of civilization. It was greatest before there was any civilization."[16] In the first stage of cultural development, discussed earlier, sexual impulse may be freely exercised without regard to procreation. "The sexual instinct . . . does not originally serve the purposes of procreation, but has as its aim the gain of particular kinds of pleasure." In the second stage, the whole of sexual impulse is suppressed "except that portion which subserves procreation." It is this second stage, it will be remembered, that Freud takes "as our standard." His standard is a mean between extremes, and for Freud it is the desired goal. In the third stage, only "*legitimate* procreation is allowed as a sexual aim. This third stage represents our 'civilized' sexual morality."[17]

Throughout his discussions of sexual morality, Freud qualifies "civilized" in this manner, indicating that he finds it uncivilized, or supercivilized, which comes to the same thing. His objection springs from his observation that third-stage morality impairs the health and efficiency of a significant proportion of individuals. "Ultimately this injury . . . may reach such a pitch that the 'civilized' aim and end will itself be indirectly endangered." The injurious influence of culture "reduces itself in all essentials to the undue suppression of the sexual life." The requirement that everyone shall have the same sexual standard is a source of "obvious injustice," because it "disregards dissimilarities . . . and cuts off a fair number of people from sexual enjoyment."[18]

Freud held these opinions unbudgingly during his entire career, from his early " 'Civilized' Sexual Morality and Modern Nervousness" to such later works as *Civilization and Its Discontents*. He treated the individual victims of these cultural trends in his clinical practice, and found three corresponding stages of individual development. The individual passes from autoerotism to object love, and "from the autonomy of the erotogenic zones to the sublimation of these under the primacy of the genitals, which come into the service of procreation." During this process, a large portion of sexual excitation is checked "as being useless for the reproductive function, and in favorable cases is diverted to sublimation."[19] Since sublimation was the only means by which Freud perceived man to be humanitarian or even useful to himself or society, he was bound to find sublimation a favorable phenomenon. The necessity for the greater portion of the libidinal energy to be available for sublimation also bound him to a reproductive model of health.

Thus far, the individual/cultural analogy functions as a pair of parallel but separate progressions. What joins them is the familial situation, and the father in particular. Civilization originally demanded renunciation from each individual. "It is chiefly family feeling, with its erotic roots, which has induced the individual to make this renunciation."[20] Each person's abstention was offered to the divinity as a sacrifice, and the first "divinity" who demanded the sacrifice was the father. "God is in every case modeled after the father." The superego is the voice of God, a literal God the Father. According to Freud, religious need is derived from infant and childhood helplessness.

"The authority of the father . . . is introjected into the ego and there forms the kernel of the superego, which takes its severity from the father, perpetuates his prohibition against incest, and ensures the ego against a recurrence of the libidinal object-cathexis."[21] Elsewhere, Freud modified this statement of the source of severity in the superego, which arises from the strength of the individual's aggressive impulses toward the father as well as from the father's severity. The feeling of guilt arises before the formation of the superego as the result of simple fear of the father's authority. It is only in internalized form that it properly belongs to the functions of the superego. Religion exploits and reproduces the sense of guilt; religious authorities "claim to redeem mankind from this sense of guilt, which they call Sin." The path to redemption is narrow, and the technique of obtaining redemption "consists in depressing the value of life and distorting the picture of the real world in a delusional manner—which presupposes an intimidation of the intelligence."[22]

One might open almost any page of Blake's collected works and find succinct statements that reveal his knowledge of all of these processes. "One law for the Lion & Ox is oppression." "Those who restrain desire do so because theirs is weak enough to be restrained." "They supposed that Womans Love is Sin." The two men and minds are very different, and I do not wish to suggest that their analyses are ever identical or to eradicate the differences between them through my own analysis. Even in the closest parallels of the two men, a kind of "continental drift" is discernible. The Oedipus complex is among the closest parallels between Blake and Freud, and it is also an issue on which they differ in significant particulars.

The priests in "The Garden of Love" are cruel, prohibiting fathers who shut the gates of desire and impose a strict standard of regulation on the child. "The Garden of Love" is a symbolic treatment of the passing of the oedipal phase in the psyche of the male.

> I went to the Garden of Love,
> And saw what I never had seen:
> A Chapel was built in the midst,
> Where I used to play on the green.

For the infant and very young child, the mother is an erotic garden of love. He is not restricted in his love for her. When the oedipal son sees "what he never had seen," he is perceiving for the first time his father's prohibition against erotic desire toward the mother. Blake referred to the female genitalia as a religious shrine whenever he dealt with society under the domination of organized patriarchal religion. In *Jerusalem*, "the most evident God" is "in a hidden covert, even / In the shadows of a Woman & a secluded Holy Place" (30:32-33). A daughter of Albion "in cruelty of holiness" delights kings in her "tabernacle & her ark &

secret place" (68:14-15), and sexual intercourse in the natural world is "a pompous High Priest entering by a secret place" (69:44).

What the child has never seen was there before his birth, but his perception changes as he enters the harsh restraints of experience. He will not be permitted to "play on the green" anymore. He must henceforth sublimate erotic feeling for his mother and venerate her from a respectful distance as an object of worship.

> And the gates of this Chapel were shut,
> Thou shalt not. writ over the door.

"Thou shalt not" is writ over the door by the father, and translates into this prohibition: You cannot marry your mother, and you may not even continue to desire her. The boy perceives that punishment for continued erotic impulse toward the mother will be loss of the offending party, the penis. The castration complex in the male child signals the resolution of the oedipal situation. The speaker of the poem returns to the garden of love,

> And I saw it was filled with graves,
> And tombstones where flowers should be.

From this time forward in the boy's libidinal development, the mother's genitalia are death, the womb transformed into tomb. She is dead to him as a sexual object, and he fears his own death as punishment for desiring her. The child resents this new restriction, which Blake expresses by the speaker's notion that flowers should still be there.

> And Priests in black gowns were walking their rounds,
> And binding with briars my joys & desires.

At the end the father shows himself in the garb of priest. The priests "walk their rounds"; in other words, the father demonstrates his possession of the mother. His color is appropriately black because this is the first time the boy must clearly face the prospect of his own death. The joys and desires are Freud's wishes, and the primal wish of the child is always for sexual union with the parent of the opposite sex.

This is not a comprehensive reading of the text, however. "The Garden of Love" deals with all repression of desire through organized religion. The poem is broadly conceived to allow for analogy of the individual and culture. The priests are really priests, and the chapel is a place of worship. The garden of love in its original state corresponds to the first stage of cultural as well as individual development, in which sexual impulse is freely expressed. And sexual impulse represents and includes all desire, "only one must conceive of the sexual function in its true range."[23] That is Freud speaking, but it could as well have been Blake. Far from being reductive, psychoanalytic reading that demonstrates that Blake was dealing with early sexual material, and knew exactly what he was doing, opens rather than closes the poem's range of significance. The final lines express Freud's third stage of cultural development, in which civilized sexual morality demands renunciation of instinctual pleasure. The priest is the mediator between the father of the familial situation and the God-Father of Christianity.

In Freudian theory, the severity of the father is the product of his own superego formation, in which internalized prohibitions cement an identification with his own father. In Blake's *Songs of Experience* the priest is the mediator not only between individual and culture but also between father and son. Fathers are victims as well as victimizers; the priest figure represents the father's superego as well as his imposition of superego formation on his son. The superego is "a memorial to the former weakness and dependence of the ego, and the mature ego remains subject to its domination. As the child was once compelled to obey its parents, so the ego submits to the categorical imperative pronounced by its superego."[24]

"A Little Boy Lost" contains two intergenerational confrontations, the first between father and son, the second between father and priest. The son has not developed the "normal" deference to his father, and because he is not a product of perfected superego development, he sees all of the things that normally become repressed. The son confronts his father with the narcissism of all object love.

> Nought loves another as itself
> Nor venerates another so.
> Nor is it possible to Thought
> A greater than it self to know:

The son admits that he cannot love his father with the ultimately self-effacing respect that society demands, and at the same time casts doubt on the depth of the father's love for the son. The speaker of this poem, like that of "The School Boy," is a visionary. He is an experienced innocent who perceives the latent content of manifest feeling.

> And Father, how can I love you,
> Or any of my brothers more?
> I love you like the little bird
> That picks up crumbs around the door.

The speaker confronts the father with the fact that his affection is not freely given, but is the result of his helplessness and dependency in the family situation. Under this programmatic process of retarded development in civilized society, maturation is bound to take the course Freud described. What passes for love is dependence and fear.

At this point in the poem, the father might be expected to answer, but instead, the priest enters, and "In trembling zeal he seiz'd his hair." The priest of "our most holy mystery" binds the child in an "iron chain" and burns him "in a holy place." The boy atones with his life for the clarity of his vision. Father and mother both weep while the priest carries out his holy office. The punishment seems brutal and excessive, so the son's sin must be, and is, more serious than it appears on the surface. By

uncovering the sources of "love" in the family, the boy has uncovered the "mystery" of organized religion as well. God is the
father writ large, and love for God is the product of fear and
dependence; thus the priest takes over the function of punishment, which normally devolves on the father. Again Blake
makes explicit the parallel between the individual and culture,
by having a cultural representative interfere in what seems to be
only a domestic matter.

The father is a silent partner in the death of his child; he
weeps and appears helpless, guileless, and guiltless. This is
Blake's exposition of the father's own psychic drama. On one
level, he is the victim of the priest, who has taken his son from
him without permission. The priest is an abstraction of patriarchal authority, so that the boy's father is only a son with respect
to the priest. The priest represents the severity of the father's own
father. But the father of the poem has introjected *his* father's
prohibitions and restrictions, else he would not allow the priest
to kill his son. His repressed aggressiveness toward his own
father is reflected in the severity of his superego. The confrontation between father and son in the first verse is a reenactment of
the father's own confrontation, which he desired but never
enacted—because if he had, he too would be dead. His son's
aggressiveness and resentment toward him replay his toward his
own father, which he has repressed. The priest who seems a
separate character is actually the father's own superego demand-
ing enforcement of the categorical imperative. That categorical
imperative makes the father simultaneous victim and victimizer.
The death of the boy may be literal, or it may be the symbolic
equivalent of the "normal" outcome of the child's expression of
hostility toward the father in the Freudian model: threatened
death in the form of the castration complex, followed by enforced formation of the boy's own superego. That, for Blake, is
equivalent to murder.

In "A Little Girl Lost," the formation of the superego in the
female and the oedipal relationship between father and daughter are explored according to the same formula. A "youthful

pair" met in a "garden bright" where light "had just removed the curtains of night"; that is, they awoke to puberty after latency, and unearthed repressed desire. They were free to "play," to discover each other sexually, because "parents were afar." The children of innocence played on the green in full sight of their parents, who watched them with nostalgic pride and affection. But in order for this new kind of play to occur, parents must be absent. The sexual play is itself innocent, but the parental perception of it is corrupt. Parents displace their own corrupt perception and project moral imperatives onto activities that are inherently innocent.

The maiden "soon forgot her fear," and the pair were free. But like Thel, these children were caught between innocence and experience; the maid forgot her fear, but forgetting suggests she had to overcome it. She was already the victim of repression, but in this case was able to repress the prohibition instead of the impulse. The two agreed to meet in the night, and that pact confirmed their knowledge that they were engaging in forbidden activity.

> To her father white
> Came the maiden bright:
> But his loving look,
> Like the holy book,
> All her tender limbs with terror shook.
>
> Ona! pale and weak!
> To thy father speak!
> O the trembling fear!
> O the dismal care!
> That shakes the blossoms of my hoary hair.

The girls says not a word. The father does not specify what he fears. All that matters remains unspoken, unwritten, and unspecified. But the reader knows instantly, I think, what is at issue, as do Ona and her father. She has been engaging in sexual activity which she knows is "wrong,"—that is, prohibited by her father—even if he has never said a specific word on the subject.

She must recognize this prohibition partly in consequence of her own oepidal phase, in which her father would have rejected her as a sexual partner. She internalized that rejection as a prohibition. As a pubertal woman, she is in the limbo between sexual maturity and the legitimate expression of sexuality in marriage. The girl's first erotic impulses toward the father are now prohibited, but so are any other cathexes she might develop in the effort to redirect and express those impulses.

Ona's automatic guilty response the moment she sees her father is the proof that she has largely internalized his prohibitions—in other words, superego formation is nearly complete. The fear she "forgot" on the green with her lover is the measure of her "progress" in that formation. The absence of her father is not quite adequate to make her refrain, but his "look" is enough to recall with force what she has forgotten. He need say nothing to produce the guilty response. In more precise terms, her response is largely one of shame. It is his "loving look" that disarms and finally terrifies her. (Even Freud's superego is not entirely negative-prohibitive, for it includes the internalization of loving relations.)

That "loving look" is shorthand for a situation far more complex than it appears on the surface, because it involves his love for her as well as hers for him. Her response is terror, because what she faces in his eye is the dread of incest. Their terror becomes mutual because their repressed fear and desire are also mutual. She comes to her father, her first object of desire toward the opposite sex, fresh from a sexual encounter. Because her desire toward other objects has not been sanctioned, the quality of the forbidden that attaches to any sexual encounter is the unconscious equivalent of the forbidden nature of the first and primal desire. Blake summarizes the connection between the father and religion again in a single simile. The father's loving look is "like the holy book," which proscribes gratification of desire.

One other characteristic quality of superego formation suggests that Ona's incestuous desire is recalled by the loving look. The superego is as irrational as the id, for its function is to battle id impulse. "Whereas the ego is essentially the representative of the external world . . . the superego stands in contrast to it as the representative of the internal world, of the id."[25] The superego does not dally about, prohibiting incidental passions. It always goes right to the heart of the matter, and its ruthless violence is reserved for the most comprehensive and fundamental id impulses, which are both sexual and aggressive. Ona's response seems almost ridiculous unless more than a conscious and consciously broken rule is at issue. She shakes with terror in front of her kindly old father, and becomes "pale and weak." She is also responding to yet another forbidden impulse, her aggressive and hostile feelings toward the father for presenting prohibitions in the first place, which produced the fear her lover overcame. "When an instinctual trend undergoes repression, its libidinal elements are turned into symptoms, and its aggressive components into a sense of guilt."[26] Ona's physical transformations in the presence of her father are symptoms. It might at first seem adequate to say that her actions with the boy were sufficient to explain them. But the "instinctual trend" that has undergone repression is not the desire for the boy after all, for she has overcome that repression.

Ona's father responds almost as strongly as she. He is afraid, and part of his fear is his own response to Ona's sexuality. He is old, and his daughter's youthful eroticism, which is so apparent to both, is a source of "dismal care" for him. It makes him "tremble." If she has made love with a boy, she has defied his prohibition and been unfaithful to him as well. Any father's refusal to let a daughter express her sexuality toward men other than himself is partly a refusal to let her give up the original cathexis toward him, even if he has prohibited it.

His care and fear shake the "blossoms" of his hoary hair. Blossoms are flowering buds, and the original bud of his own sexual desire toward his mother is inevitably replayed in his relationship with wife and daughter. The wife, Ona's mother, is absent in the poem. Blake might have had Ona appear to both parents, as he does in many of the songs of experience where parents weep together or are addressed as a unit. His choice of the lone father in "A Little Girl Lost" is, I believe, deliberate. It gives him the opportunity to express the repressed erotic components of the father–daughter bond. Ona's absentee mother *is* present. She is Ona.

With the exceptions of a very few speakers, the personae who inhabit the world of experience are not conscious of the psychic processes they enact. "I Dreamt a Dream! what can it mean?" expresses the level of self-awareness of many of the speakers. Blake ends *Songs of Experience* with "The Voice of the Ancient Bard," who tells the "youth of delight" that "Folly is an endless maze."

> Tangled roots perplex her ways,
> How many have fallen there!
> They stumble all night over the bones of the dead;
> And feel they know not what but care;
> And wish to lead others when they should be led.

The voice warns the young that their parents, and many of their own number, are grappling with their dead, and with their dying passions. The "tangled roots" are the sources of psychic conflict through which people thread their way during life, living as if in a dream of death.

"How many have fallen there!" According to Freud, "the beginnings of religion, ethics, society and art meet in the Oedipus complex."[27] Within the context of the oedipal configuration, Freud's repeated remonstrance that sexuality must be understood "in its true range" became particularly important. Freud's statements about oedipal resonance are ridiculous if sexuality is defined in a strictly genital sense, or even in a strictly bodily sense. Freud meant the Oedipus complex to be understood as a complicated series of psychic relationships and events by means of which a person learns how to become a member of society.

The songs of experience deal implicitly with family romance, but they are only Blake's first words on the specific aspect of it that has since been labeled the Oedipus complex. My claim that Blake anticipated all of the fundamentals of Freudian theory cannot be completed without intensive explication of Blake's convictions on this issue, and at first glance it might seem that a good deal of judicious fudging might be necessary to establish that Blake invested the Oedipus complex with a resonance in any way comparable to its position in Freudian theory. "A Little Girl Lost" and "The Garden of Love" demonstrate that Blake was well aware of oedipal configurations, but my reading admittedly gains some of its strength from inference. The songs of experience are adequate indicators of the breadth of Blake's knowledge of the oedipal process; but perhaps they do not demonstrate the depth of that knowledge. Blake's adumbration of the Oedipus complex in *The First Book of Urizen* and *The Four Zoas* answers to the need for depth and detail in Blake's analysis of oedipal conflict.

Blake's interpretation of psychohistorical data was somewhat different from Freud's, as "A Little Girl Lost" indicates. For Freud, the oedipal struggle was the child's struggle. Freud seldom mentioned sexual desire for the child on the part of the parent, or sexual jealousy as a normal component of the parental role in the drama. Man must face the thought of incest "with mother or sister" in order to come to terms with sexuality and with cultural pressure; he does not confront the thought of incest with his daughter. After Freud discovered that his early female patients had fantacized seductions by fathers or father figures, he abandoned what then seemed to him an unfruitful line of inquiry. He did not deny the reality of seduction by fathers; he simply ignored it.

The sexual union of fathers and daughters in Blake's major prophecies is a matter of mutual passion. In comprehensive terms, Blake interpreted the entire oedipal situation as a "problem" for both parent and child. (Marriage to Oedipus is Jocasta's tragedy as well as her son's. She hangs herself.) In fact, it may be accurate to say that Blake perceived it as originally the problem of the parent, which the parent then communicates to the child.

I confine the present discussion to the mother–son relationship and its attendant effects on the father. This was, of course, the manifestation of the complex that Freud developed most fully:

> At a very early age the little boy develops an object-cathexis of his *mother*, which originally related to the mother's breast and is the earliest instance of an object-choice on the anaclitic model; his *father* the boy deals with by identifying himself with him. For a time these two relationships exist side by side, until the sexual wishes in regard to the mother become more intense and the father is perceived as an obstacle to them; this gives rise to the Oedipus complex. The identification with the father then takes on a hostile coloring and changes into a wish to get rid of the father in order to take his place with the mother. Henceforward the relation to the father is ambivalent; it seems as if the ambivalence inherent in the identification from the beginning had become manifest. An ambivalent attitude to the father and an object-relation of a purely affectionate kind to the mother make up the content of the simple positive Oedipus complex in the boy.[28]

The words "simple" and "positive" are important. Freud was not always so schematic in describing a situation to which he attributed the beginnings of acculturation, but the summary version is the most appropriate for this necessarily limited context. Freud discusses the situation from a chronologically developmental point of view; it is an emphasis rather than an oversight that he perceives it entirely in terms of the way a child feels and thinks.

In *The First Book of Urizen*, Blake's mythic giants are beginning to emerge as representatives of psychic processes and entities that Blake believed to be universal, and the events they enact are universal human phenomena. In Chapter VII of *Urizen*, the first woman, Enitharmon, and the first man, poet-prophet Los, are faced with the task of primal parenting. Their child, Orc, is the first human issue of a union between man and woman. He remains less a character than a principle in Blake's later works, and he represents the energetic spirit of revolution against oppression. From his earliest appearance in Blake's work, Orc is actively antagonistic to passivity, reason, and law.

The so-called Orc cycle begins with a principle of revolution, but eventually wears itself out through what would be called "identification with the aggressor" in psychoanalytic terms. The Orc force diminishes to a remnant of its original energy and institutes another repressive phase, which must in turn be overthrown by a new embodiment of the original energy it forfeited. When repressed, Orc energy turns into revolutionary war in its positive manifestation, or Satanic antienergy in its negative manifestation. Again, and as always in Blake, the sociohistorical situation has its analogues, and ultimately its prototypes, in the familial, personal, individual context from which the cultural is abstracted. Sons grow into fathers of their own sons, the generational conflict writ large. The first part of the Orc cycle corresponds to the first phases of family romance. The story of the first family is Blake's backreading of history and his explanation of culture.

This first birth is painful because it is conceived in pain. Los has undergone a separation not only from Urizen but also from his feminine portion, Enitharmon. The mating of Los and Enitharmon is a desperate attempt to reunify the fragments of wholeness, and the best they can do is to produce a third being who is part of them both, but only part. The interests of parents in their issue thus become a struggle between them for ascendancy, a struggle in which the welfare of the child is not the main consideration. Orc mediates the ego needs of his mother and father, whose fall from original wholeness produces divided interests as well as a divided image.

> Eternity shudder'd when they saw,
> Man begetting his likeness,
> On his own divided image.
> [*The First Book of Urizen* 19:14–16]

Parenting is the final stage of removal from eternal wholeness, for it makes psychic separation concrete. It commits people to abandon genuine unification, and compels them to settle for the shadow of their original desire for wholeness. That, for Blake, is a definition of "procreation."

The father immediately relinquishes the child to the mother, and thereby accepts a secondary role in parenting at the beginning of the child's life.

> No more Los beheld Eternity.
> 11. In his hands he siez'd the infant
> He bathed him in springs of sorrow
> He gave him to Enitharmon.
>
> [*The First Book of Urizen* 20:2–5]

Orc grows "fed with milk of Enitharmon." Instead of enjoying fatherhood, Los experiences it in "sorrow and pain." The resentment he feels at being put aside (or voluntarily putting himself aside) surfaces as a generalized feeling of deprivation that will later manifest itself as aggression toward the child. In the extended version of the story in *The Four Zoas,* the symbiotic solipsism inherent in the mother–child diad is more explicit. "Enitharmon nursd her fiery child in the dark deeps / Sitting in darkness" (59:25–26). Los must attempt to "awaken" Enitharmon from the sleeplike state induced by nursing.

The source of Los's anguish remains unclear in *The First Book of Urizen*, but in *The Four Zoas* Blake is far less cryptic. "For now he feard Eternal Death & uttermost Extinction" (60:2). The meaning of the child's birth is no secret to Los in the longer text. He knows his son will be his executioner, if not by rebelling, then merely by living and growing strong while his father grows old and weak. Los's expression of fear is followed immediately by the building of Golgonooza, the city of art, an evidence that Blake well understood the process of sublimation. Los diverts the aim of his aggression, changes its content, and converts his resentment and sexual frustration into cultural achievement. Yet the fear is never dispelled.

> But when fourteen summers & winters had revolved over
> Their solemn habitation Los beheld the ruddy boy
> Embracing his bright mother & beheld malignant fires
> In his young eyes discerning plain that Orc plotted his death
> [*The Four Zoas* 60:6–9]

Blake chooses a ripe adolescence for the age of the child in the overt stage of oedipal struggle, and such a vast departure from the Freudian formulation might well seem to indicate that Blake is mythologizing another phenomenon altogether. Yet Blake elsewhere demonstrated his knowledge, even his advocacy, of infantile sexuality. It appears as if he overlooked an opportunity to engage in deeper analysis of the family romance. But in fact Blake conflated at least two "events," one psychic and one social, by placing the oedipal conflict in the pubertal stage, for it made the story intelligible in terms of Blake's historical-cycle symbolism. The child of five is not a manifest threat to the power and authority of the father, and he is still helpless to express his ambivalence in any way that might change the power structure of the family unit or the larger cultural unit. At puberty the son becomes heir to sexual prowess and to real power, and he then presents a genuine threat to the father. Even though the child feels sexual urges toward the mother and resentment toward the father when he is younger, there is virtually nothing he can do about it until he comes into man's estate. Similarly, the father who becomes consciously aware of the source of his sadness and fear when the boy reaches puberty is expressing what he had felt since the child was an infant.

The action that precipitates Los's overt fear of his son is the pubertal boy's sexual relationship to the mother. The mother represents all women for the son and for the father, and the boy's emerging sexual prowess is a signal to the father that he, the father, is no longer the only bull in the territory. The "malignant fires" Los beholds in Orc's eyes are an open acknowledgment that the child hates his father and perceives him as a sexual competitor. What Freud called the wish to "get rid of the father" is here an explicit plot to murder the father—from the father's point of view. This sequence of psychic events is exactly analogous to Freud's description of mental process in the boy child. But Freud formulated the workings of the Oedipus complex long after he had himself become a father, literally and symbolically. He intended to reveal the feelings of a child, but if one reads the situation in a Blakean manner, it might be said that Freud could hardly avoid revealing his own feelings as well.

In Blake's story the original process takes place, then, in the mind of the father as well as in the mind of the son—perhaps, even, in the mind of the father instead of in the mind of the son. It is true that Orc will grow into a principle of revolutionary energy, but that development may be largely determined by the father's behavior toward him. The narrator is careful to describe the psychic constituents entirely from Los's perspective, and in Blake's mythology, fact is always in the eye of the beholder. Los beholds what he fears—the malignant fires, the death wish, the plot—and like all Blakean characters, he becomes what he beholds. What he beholds may be, in turn, only a projection of his own feelings. Whether Los merely reflects or actually creates Orc's antagonistic feelings is a question Blake's diction leaves deliberately open.

Immediately following Los's perception of Orc's plot against him, "grief rose upon his ruddy brows." The word "ruddy," applied to Orc a few lines earlier, intensifies the ironic identification of father and son.

> . . . a tightening girdle grew
> Around his bosom like a bloody cord. in secret sobs
> He burst it, but next morn another girdle succeeds
> Around his bosom. Every day he viewd the fiery youth
> With silent fear & his immortal cheeks grew deadly pale
> Till many a morn & many a night passd over in dire woe
> Forming a girdle in the day & bursting it at night . . .
> [*The Four Zoas* 60:10–16]

Blake calls Los's "uncouth plague" the "Chain of Jealousy." Blake's engraving for the story in *The First Book of Urizen* is a remarkable one for any era, but especially for a pre-Freudian one. Enitharmon stands naked next to Los, with the adolescent, naked Orc entwined about her. Orc's gaze is directed upward toward his mother, and his mouth nearly touches her breast. Orc and Enitharmon engage in the dance of mother–son love, their limbs nearly melted together, their skin coloring similar to each other's and sharply differentiated from Los's.

Orc shows no consciousness of his father's existence. He attempts to compel his mother's entire attention, and almost, but
not quite, succeeds. Enitharmon's body is entirely involved in the
embrace, but she turns her face slightly toward Los. Her gaze is
diverted from Orc so that she appears to be looking abstractedly
at both, or at neither. She is divided in her affection for son and
for husband, and the struggle shows in her face, but with no
resolution. Los stands beside them, his body turned slightly
away, but his face turned toward the boy's face reaching for the
mother's breast. In all other portrayals, Los is shown as young,
vigorous, and energetic, but here he is the image of Urizen,
bearded, old, and careworn. A huge red chain hangs from his
body and bends him slightly with its weight. He leans against his
hammer and anvil, the tools of his trade, which he is about to
convert into weapons to employ against Orc.

> He siezd the boy in his immortal hands
> While Enitharmon followed him weeping in dismal woe
> Up to the iron mountain top & there the Jealous chain
> Fell from his bosom on the mountain. The Spectre dark
> Held the fierce boy Los naild him down binding around his
> limbs
> The accursed chain O how bright Enitharmon howld & cried
> Over her son. Obdurate Los bound down her loved Joy
> [*The Four Zoas* 60:24–30]

The Promethean parallel is probably deliberate, for Orc has
also stolen fire from the gods, the fire of sexual passion. The
chain of jealousy falls from Los because he thinks to free himself
from its source by binding the child who threatens his manhood
and authority. It is important to note that Los uses the chain of
jealousy itself to tie down the child, for by that action he trans-
fers his jealousy to the child. It is at this point that Blake's myth
joins Freud's. As is so often the case, Blake's etiology begins the
cause-and-effect sequence one step earlier in psychic time. The
father is soon sorry for his premature aggression toward the son,
who is, after all, a part of himself. When Los returns to his city of

Golgonooza, he and Enitharmon "felt all the sorrow Parents feel." Los repents immediately, "parental love" returns, and he determines to free Orc even at the cost of his own life. But he cannot free Orc, for Orc's limbs have "strucken root" in the rock.

> Fibres had from the Chain of Jealousy inwove themselves
> In a swift vegetation round the rock & round the Cave
> And over the immortal limbs of the terrible fiery boy
> In vain they strove now to unchain.
>
> [*The Four Zoas* 62:23–26]

The chain roots not only into the rock, but also "beneath the Earth / Even to the Center," becoming one with Orc, "a living chain" (63:1–3). The generational conflict between father and son is hereafter a given in human history. Blake's last word on the misadventures of Los and Enitharmon as a result of botching the hugely significant job of primal parenting is sadly comprehensive. "All their lamentations / I write not here but all their after life was lamentation" (63:8–9). Anyone who doubts that a predecessor of Freud could have invested the oedipal situation with such "Freudian" resonance might ponder that statement. In both versions of the story, Los's abortive attempt to free Orc is immediately succeeded by the formation of cultural institutions and organized religion. We are again with Freud: "The beginnings of religion, ethics, society and art meet in the Oedipus complex."

The story of Los, Orc, and Enitharmon is Blake's *Totem and Taboo* as well as his exploration of family romance. Orc is hailed "Luvah King of Love" at his birth (58:22). In Blake's mythology, Luvah is the Zoa of sexual passion. His birth in the form of Orc is the first in a series of incarnations that ultimately ends with the birth of Christ. The Luvah principle is an eternal one of love, but when suppressed it is converted into hate. "When Luvah in Orc became a Serpent, he des[c]ended into / That State calld Satan" (115:26–27). The "King of Love" is also the "King of rage & death." The son's love for the father turns into resentment. Freud succinctly expressed this process in "Instincts and Their

Vicissitudes": "The reversal of content is found in the single instance of the change of love into hate."[29] Christ can end the cycle of father–son dispute by incarnating Luvah's original state of love and forgiveness, of a brotherhood in which all men are in fraternal relation to each other, instead of in generational conflict. But although Christ brings peace, he also brings a sword to kill the oppressive father, Jehovah. That should end the problem, but of course it does not. Christ is crucified, and his murder is another sexual crime, a family tragedy of passion and lust.

In *Totem and Taboo*, the primal crime is patricide; in Blake's myth, the primal crime is filicide. Patricide *follows* filicide as a necessary consequence, for the chain of jealousy that originated with the father is passed to the son. And filicide is ultimately suicide, for Los requires the assistance of the spectre (self-murder) in order to chain Orc. Los gives the spectre "sternest charge over the howling fiend" after he is chained (61:9). Los is "immortal," but he has convinced himself that he will die, and determined his own death by attempting to kill his son. The father cannot kill the son, but his effort to do so spells his own doom. Los's own self-destructive urges are his only ally in the binding of Orc.

Finally, it is not the difference in the age of the child or even the cause-and-effect sequence that makes Blake's analysis of the Oedipus complex different from Freud's. In Freud's scenario, the father is a constant principle who remains steady through all the passions of the child. Freud taught us all how childish we remain throughout adult life, but the father in the oedipal struggle and in the primal horde has none of the child in him; or at any rate, Freud was not concerned to reveal the child hidden within the father. Perhaps he saw the issue as irrelevant; perhaps he did not see the issue at all. For Blake, that issue constituted perhaps more than half of the problem. Father and son are both passionately involved in the oedipal struggle, and the stakes are fully as great for both parties. It is a life-and-death struggle, and it is a necessary one. "Without Contraries is no progression. Attraction and Repulsion, Reason and Energy, Love and Hate, are necessary to Human existence." We arrive, by a circuitous route, at *The Marriage of Heaven and Hell*.

Songs of Experience deals with the formation of culture and religion from the individual's perspective in the family unit. The oedipal configuration in *The First Book of Urizen* and *The Four Zoas* conflates the familial and the cultural. *The Marriage of Heaven and Hell*, published in 1793 (before the *Songs*) studies the same phenomena on the cosmic scale. The universal tensions Blake calls contraries are abstracted by society into morality.

> From these contraries spring what the religious call
> Good & Evil. Good is the passive that obeys Reason.
> Evil is the active springing from energy.
> Good is Heaven. Evil is Hell.
> [*The Marriage of Heaven and Hell*, Plate 3]

Even Freud was never more succinct. Id impulses are designated as evil by society because their indulgence would retard the process of sublimation by which culture achieves its ends. "Energy" is Blake's id, and "the passive that obeys Reason" is the conservative trend in culture. It obeys Reason only at a great expenditure of energy, for unruly impulses must be constantly kept passive, latent, repressed. Good consists in obedience to the father in the family and to law and religion in society.

The *Marriage* says that all bibles and sacred codes teach falsehoods, among which is "that God will torment Man in Eternity for following his energies" (Plate 4). This God is the same as Freud's God, who metes out punishment and reward for renunciation and sacrifice. "Those who restrain desire do so because theirs is weak enough to restrain; and the restrainer or reason usurps its place and governs the unwilling. And being restrained it by degrees becomes passive till it is only the shadow of desire" (Plate 5).

Freud calls the restraints of morality unjust for much the same reason. The demand is one that "one person can attain without effort, whereas it imposes on another the severest mental sacrifices."[30] All men are originally the "unwilling" in Blake and

Freud. "What makes itself felt in a human community as a desire for freedom . . . may (also) spring from the remains of their original personality, which is still untamed by civilization."[31] The restraint works with the majority, yielding Blake's "shadow of desire" and Freud's neurotic personality, for whom "the return of the repressed" is experienced as illness.

When Blake's proverbs on desire are read against a backdrop of Freud's formulations on neurosis in society, their intent becomes clear. Undue suppression of sexuality is responsible for neurosis. "He who desires but acts not breeds pestilence" becomes intelligible as a cultural norm. The "pestilence" is neurosis in culture. Anyone who has ever tried to explain the sense of "Sooner murder an infant in its cradle than nurse unacted desire" might be grateful for Freud's support of what seems an inexplicably cruel metaphor. The human infant is murdered in its cradle when desire is unacted and therefore repressed, and the collective trend of nursing unacted desire in society kills the aim of human happiness, which ought to be the goal of civilization if it is to have any advantage whatever over an uncivilized state. "Damn. braces: Bless relaxes." "Expect poison from the standing water." "The road of excess leads to the palace of wisdom." "The tygers of wrath are wiser than the horses of instruction." "Prisons are built with stones of Law, Brothels with bricks of Religion."

That last proverb conflates and summarizes the fundamentals of Freud's findings on culture. Excessive strictness of law creates crime through suppression of instinct beyond a level the individual can tolerate. "No individual can keep these Laws, for they are death / To every energy of man" (*Jerusalem* 31:11–12). (If the capital *L* were removed from Laws and if the line break were absent, I wonder whether any student of Freud and Blake could guess which one had said it.) Religion creates prostitution by forbidding the indulgence of sexual appetite until marriage, and even after.

For Blake, the conflagration "will come to pass by an improvement of sensual enjoyment." Freud would agree that immediate gratification of impulse would bring about the destruction of the civilized world. But he would not advise it and would be horrified at the prospect. Blake thought civilization, as constituted, not worth the trouble necessary to maintain it. The revolution that destroys it will be a happy and holy one in which everything will "appear infinite" instead of "finite & corrupt." For Freud, the world appears finite and corrupt too, but its destruction would leave nothing of infinite value. It would leave nothing at all.

The creation of religion on the cultural level in *The Marriage of Heaven and Hell* is a derivative of the projective process. "The ancient Poets animated all sensible objects with Gods or Geniuses." They were "mental deities," but eventually a system was formed by abstraction of the deities from their objects. "Thus began Priesthood." The process is analogous to Freud's in *Totem and Taboo*. "Thus men forgot that All deities reside in the human breast." "Forgot" has much the same content as "repressed." The original mental deities were concentrated in the person of the father, and from the father of the family the God of culture was abstracted. "Primitive man," according to Freud, "transferred the structural relations of his own psyche to the outer world."[32]

The Marriage of Heaven and Hell takes place on a mythic level in order to describe the contours of the holy as they took shape in the minds of men. Blake employed the concept of marriage to symbolize relationships between forces and principles, but he was equally attuned to the sociosexual relationship between men and women in his own society. He recognized marriage as the core relationship of the nuclear family, and therefore a cornerstone of civilization. It is to Blake's assessment of marriage that I now turn.

4. Marriage: *Visions of the Daughters of Albion*

Oothoon, Bromion, and Theotormon. From William Blake, *Visions of the Daughters of Albion*, Frontispiece (1793). Relief etching.
The Tate Gallery, London.

In his poetics of marriage, Blake analyzed the relationship between masculine and feminine in persons and in principles. Blake's marriage ideal, as expressed especially in *Jerusalem,* was a mutually responsible and mutually loving covenant relationship, but the reality he perceived bore little similarity to his ideal. *Visions of the Daughters of Albion* is another marriage of heaven and hell, and through it Blake analyzed "normal" sexual development in male and female far more fully than in *Songs of Innocence* and *Songs of Experience.* In the *Songs,* Blake's knowledge of psychic process must be inferred; in *Visions,* he presents a coherent theory of psychic development in the sexes.

The drama is operatic: passionate, hopeless, tragic, and simple. The visionary poet-prophet of *Visions* is Oothoon, a virgin who awakens to sexual maturity and acts on her impulses instead of repressing them, as Thel did. Oothoon's encounter with a flower nymph in the opening passages of *Visions* represents her conscious decision to become a sexual being. The marigold tells Oothoon that she may pluck, and "another flower shall spring, because the soul of sweet delight / Can never pass away" (1:9–10). Oothoon places the plucked flower "here to glow between my breasts," literally wearing her newly discovered sexuality on her body as she flies to her lover, Theotormon. Oothoon's conversation with nature, like Thel's, is a conversation with herself, this time with the flower of her own desire.

Bromion, a relentlessly cruel representative of patriarchal law, intercepts Oothoon and rapes her. This most dramatic external event of the poem takes place in one bare line. "Bromion rent her with his thunders" (1:16). The remainder of the action is psychic and consists of lamentations by the three characters:

127

Oothoon, the victim and visionary; Theotormon, the jealous and unforgiving "husband" figure; and Bromion, the oppressor. Bromion taunts Theotormon with his conquest. "Now thou maist marry Bromion's harlot, and protect the child / Of Bromion's rage" (2:1–2). Theotormon accepts Bromion's judgment of Oothoon, but Oothoon refuses to accept the status of fallen woman and vainly attempts to persuade both of her male oppressors to consider why and how they condemn her. The males remain obdurate, and the poem closes with continued lamentation. Oothoon and Bromion are bound back to back by the act between them. Theotormon remains absorbed in his own jealousy, and will not free himself or Oothoon.

Oothoon listens to Theotormon's lament, "Tell me what is the night or day to one o'erflowed with woe?" and to Bromion's equally unproductive "Is there not one law for both the lion and the ox?" Oothoon penetrates the single source of Theotormon's jealousy and Bromion's cruelty:

> O Urizen! Creator of men! mistaken demon of heaven:
> Thy joys are tears! thy labour vain, to form men to thine
>   image.
> How can one joy absorb another? are not different joys
> Holy, eternal, infinite! and each joy is a Love.
>   [*Visions of the Daughters of Albion* 5:3–6]

Urizen is Jehovah/Nobodaddy, the God of Judaic law and of Christian patriarchy, not the God of love and brotherhood. The law that regulates the behavior of all people defines love as possession, and the demand that a woman shall enter marriage as a virgin is the perfect expression of possessiveness masquerading as love. Freud writes, "The demand that the girl shall bring with her into marriage with one man no memory of sexual relations with another is after all nothing but a logical consequence of the exclusive right of possession over a woman which is the essence of monogamy—it is but an extension of this monopoly on to the past."[1]

Freud does not speculate deeply on the relationship between

possessiveness and love, but he does acknowledge that "we must begin to love in order that we may not fall ill, and we must fall ill if, in consequence of frustration, we cannot love."[2] Blake was convinced that normal sexual development made love impossible, with the result that in the most basic love relationship on which society is founded, nearly everyone falls ill. Under the sway of Christian moral law, children grow in "nets & gins & traps" where "kings and priests may dwell,"

> Till she who burns with youth. and knows no fixed lot; is
>   bound
> In spells of law to one she loaths: and must drag the chain
> Of life, in weary lust! must chilling murderous thoughts.
>   obscure
> The clear heaven of her eternal spring? to bear the wintry
>   rage
> Of a harsh terror driv'n to madness, bound to hold a rod
> Over her shrinking shoulders all the day; & all the night
> To turn the wheel of false desire: and longings that wake her
>   womb
> To the abhorred births of cherubs in the human form
> That live a pestilence & die a meteor & are no more.
> Till the child dwell with one he hates. and do the deed he
>   loaths
> And the impure scourge force his seed into its unripe birth
> E'er yet his eyelids can behold the arrows of the day.
>   [*Visions of the Daughters of Albion* 5:21-32]

The "chain of life" the female child drags is her own life, and also the life of generate humanity, for she is forced by her fertility to become the image of nature. Her "weary lust" is the suppressed, perverted shadow of her original "burning," and the "chilling murderous thoughts" are her inevitable wishes for the death of the husband to whom she is bound. He can love no more than she, for "the bounded is loathed by its possessor" (*There Is No Natural Religion* [b], IV). His frustration engenders his "wintry rage" against her, for he too is "driv'n to madness" by loveless marriage, incessant generativity, heavy responsibility, and the hopeless task of ensuring his wife's fidelity. If they have not been brought together originally by love (and even, often, if they have), he must keep her by means of the actual foundation of their union: the force of lawful possession which binds them to each other just as Oothoon and Bromion are bound back to back in Blake's engraving for *Visions.*

The woman's "longings" are genuine because they arise from her bodily maturity, but their expression when love is absent can only be "false." The "abhorred births" of children are inevitably resented by their mother, whose life the children circumscribe through no fault of their own. Their lives, like those of their parents, will be nasty, brutish, and short. The last lines of the quotation describe the continuous, almost inherited nature of the process. The child dwells with one he hates, and that hated one is originally his mother. He marries, but can only hate his wife because he has learned to despise all women through the bond with his natural mother. He too will "do the deed he loaths," like his father before him. That deed is the sex act with the unloved and unloving wife, which results in yet another unripe birth. Blake's lament begins with the lost potential of the female and ends with the lost potential of the male, whose eyelids will never behold "the arrows of day," the gratified desire.

The diction suggests that the process may apply most specifically to young women married to older men, and that situation was certainly common in the late eighteenth century. But the husband need not be chronologically aged, and that is part of Blake's point. He refers to the conditioning that makes male children the heirs of patriarchal law from earliest youth, and which forces them directly from the position of the oppressed (the child) into the position of oppressor (the husband). The female plays the same role in marriage as does the child in the nuclear family. The male child must learn to identify with his father (his and his mother's oppressor) very early in life. Marital "love" thus takes its character directly from the prototype of parent–child interaction. Oothoon asks whether the feelings she describes can be classified as love at all.

Can that be Love, that drinks another as a sponge drinks
    water?
That clouds with jealousy his nights, with weepings all the
    day:
To spin a web of age around him. grey and hoary! dark!
Till his eyes sicken at the fruit that hangs before his sight.
Such is self-love that envies all! a creeping skeleton
With lamplike eyes watching around the frozen marriage bed.
                [*Visions of the Daughters of Albion* 7:17-22]

Jealousy and aggression in the male, resentment and frigidity
in the female: such is Blake's view of conventional matrimony. It
was also Freud's, with a slightly different emphasis:

> The uninitiated can hardly believe how rarely normal potency is to
> be found in the men, and how often frigidity in the women, among
> those married couples living under the sway of our civilized sexual
> morality; what a degree of renunciation, often for both partners, is
> associated with marriage, and of how little the marriage comes to
> consist, instead of bringing the happiness that was so ardently
> desired.[3]

Culture demands abstinence before marriage and expects that
marriage will offer enough compensation for the previous repression. But after marriage, anxiety "dissipates the physical
tenderness" and whatever degree of "mental affection" might
have existed between the partners at the outset. Under the
"spiritual disappointment" that becomes the "fate of most marriages," both partners are reduced to their preconjugal condition,
"but poorer by the loss of an illusion." Social conditioning does
not teach youth how to love at all, and "a marriage begun with
impaired capacity to love on both sides succumbs to the process
of dissolution" rapidly.[4]

Freud devotes relatively little attention to the feelings of bit-
terness, resentment, and even hate that characterize relations
between the sexes before and after marriage. He is primarily
concerned with the effects of enforced abstinence before marriage and attributes the "frustration" of man and wife to abstinence above all. Blake begins with enforced abstinence as a

premise, and backreads from it to examine its results and its "causes." In no way do their analyses conflict, however; their emphases are complementary. Of the woman who, in Blake's words, originally "burns with youth" and "knows no fixed lot," Freud writes that her "female education" forces her into a position where, "as a reward for her previous submission, there remains for her only the choice between unappeased desire, infidelity, or neurosis." Under the "present cultural standard," marriage has "long ceased to be a panacea for the . . . sufferings of women."[5] Again, Blake's exploration of the genesis and social significance of what Freud calls "female education" extends and complements that of Freud, who confessed that he wrote hesitantly about female psychology.

> Infancy, fearless, lustful, happy! nestling for delight
> In laps of pleasure; Innocence! honest, open, seeking
> The vigorous joys of morning light; open to virgin bliss,
> Who taught thee modesty, subtil modesty! child of night &
>   sleep
> When thou awakest. wilt thou dissemble all thy secret joys
> Or wert thou not, awake when all this mystery was disclos'd!
> Then com'st thou forth a modest virgin knowing to dissemble
> With nets found under thy night pillow, to catch the virgin joy
> And brand it with the name of whore; & sell it in the night,
> In silence. e'ven without a whisper, and in seeming sleep:
> Religious dreams and holy vespers, light thy smoky fires:
> Once were thy fires lighted by the eyes of honest morn
> And does my Theotormon seek this hypocrite modesty!
> This knowing, artful, secret, fearful, cautious, trembling
>   hypocrite.
> Then is Oothoon a whore indeed! and all the virgin joys
> Of life are harlots: and Theotormon is a sick mans dream
> And Oothoon is the crafty slave of selfish holiness.
>   [*Visions of the Daughters of Albion* 6:4–20]

"Who taught thee modesty?" The teacher is Urizen, the "Father of Jealousy." Freud identified the basic components of female education as submission, chastity, and abstinence;[6] in the oedipal scenario, the female child learns to behave seductively toward the father, who, even though he rejects her, implicitly demands that she express her seductiveness covertly so that she will fill the role of the marriageable virgin. The marriageable virgin must suggest to her father and to her suitors that she is actually pure and potentially passionate. The woman's function in culture is primarily sexual, for she will carry on the species through the family. She must demonstrate that she is ready for this role, while always suppressing any open expression of sexuality, which might suggest that her husband could not be sure of her purity and her capacity for fidelity. Her child must be her husband's, because it is his only means of full possession of the child, and his means to immortality.

The compromise on which the female fixes is expressed by the quality Blake calls "modesty," but the compromise is originally effected without the female's conscious knowledge. She is the child of "night and sleep," of unconsciousness. Her mother provided the example for her behavior, just as the father provided the example for the boy's behavior. She was not awake "when all this mystery was disclos'd"; or, as Blake put it in *Jerusalem,* "When the Druids demanded Chastity from Woman & all was lost" (63:25).

When the girl "comes forth," it is as the virgin who has learned the art of dissembling. Her coming forth can mean at least two things: the presentation of herself to the world as woman, and also the emergence of her consciousness as woman. Her nets are Urizen's "Nets of Religion," in which woman is always divided into the two mutual negations (not proper contraries) of whore and wife. In Blake's explication, whore and wife are artificially separated aspects of the whole woman. Recent feminist formulations of the wife/whore dichotomy view the splitting process as the product of division *by the male*. In 1793, and in the voice of a woman, Blake examined it as an action taken by the woman herself in the earliest stages of her sexual development. The father of jealousy teaches her to divide against herself, and she learns the lesson well. The woman who remains, psychically, the modest virgin throughout married life is the same woman who

"brands" virgin joy with "the name of whore." Through displacement, the wife renounces her own sexuality and banishes
the libidinous aspect of herself to the brothel. The genuine
virgin is the infant who joys in innocent passion; the cultural
virgin is a fake and a hypocrite. The ambiguous diction of the
passage conflates the identities of wife and whore, for the virgin
who "sells it in the night, / In silence. e'ven without a whisper"
behaves, ironically, much like the whore. The whore sells her sex
in the night in silence too, and endures abhorred caresses while
she "dissembles" passion.

The virgin's "seeming sleep" represents the wife's frigidity,
her avoidance of open sexuality, and also the "sleep" of her
genuine desire, which remains unexpressed. Blake elsewhere
wrote that wife and whore should be one entity for man and for
herself, and she should provide and receive "the lineaments of
gratified desire." Under civilized sexual codes, only the whore
promises gratified desire, but the promise is false, for it is passion divided from affection. The "youthful harlot's curse" in
Blake's poem "London" is the mind-forged manacle the poet
hears loudest and most clearly, and it "blights" the "marriage
hearse" because the demand for chastity murders marriage. If
men are taught to seek women who display "this hypocrite
modesty," and to value it above love, then the sexually expressive
woman is assigned the role of harlot from generation to generation, while the real whore, the "crafty slave of selfish holiness,"
wins accolades she does not deserve. Her "holiness" is her own,
but she derives it from the "holiness" of the jealous father-
husband. The growing youth is no better off than the virgin, for
he becomes only "a sick mans dream," a shadow of humanity
who must seek substitute gratification in the empty embraces of
another shadow.

Freud wrote of the demand for abstinence: "Society cannot
claim an advantage purchased by sacrifice—cannot indeed claim
any advantage whatever." The double standard of sexual
morality Blake condemns in *Visions* is, according to Freud, "the
plainest possible admission that society itself does not believe in

the possibility of adherence to those precepts which it has enjoined on its members."[7]

Freud also deals with the way in which the patterns are carried into succeeding generations, and comes to the same conclusions as Blake.

> The bad relations between the parents then stimulates the emotional life of the child, and causes it to experience intensities of love, hate, and jealousy while yet in its infancy. The strict training which tolerates no sort of expression of this precocious sexual state lends support to the forces of suppression, and the conflict at this age contains all the elements needed to cause lifelong neurosis.[8]

The content is the same as Blake's "Till the child dwell with one he hates and do the deed he loaths." It is not only the female who loathes sexuality in Blake's and Freud's views. Anyone who subjects himself to serious self-examination, says Freud, "will indubitably find that at the bottom of his heart he too regards the sexual act as something degrading, which soils and contaminates not only the body." Man and woman alike will find the origin of this attitude in the period of life in which "sexual passions were already strongly developed but in which gratification of them with an object outside the family was almost as completely prohibited as with an incestuous one."[9] We are back again to Blake's Ona in incestuous conflict with her father. Women are particularly enjoined to hate their own sexuality, and "the reaction upon them of this attitude in men" is part of the wound to their narcissism, a situation for which penis envy is the prototype but not the only manifestation. The woman develops, "like a scar, a sense of inferiority," and "shares the contempt felt by men" for her sexuality.[10] In Blake's mythology, she projects her self-disgust onto the harlot.

One ancillary development in "normal" sexuality dealt with by both Blake and Freud is masturbation, and both find in it the same potential dangers. Blake and Freud view masturbation as a substitute gratification forced on young people as the result of the demand for abstinence. Blake's virgin "shall awaken her

womb to enormous joys / In the secret shadows of her chamber."
The boy will "create an amorous image / In the shadows of his
curtains." In the light of Blake's attitudes toward other kinds of
sexuality, his disapproval seems somewhat misplaced, but it is
not the act that offends him. He does not see it as an act at all;
masturbation is actually an anti-act for Blake, one accomplished
in the dark, in silence, in the presence of an absence. It is a form
of religious abstinence.

> Are not these the places of religion? the rewards of
>   continence?
> The self enjoyings of self denial? Why dost thou seek
>   religion?
> Is it because acts are not lovely, that thou seekest solitude,
> Where the horrible darkness is impressed with reflections of
>   desire?
>   [*Visions of the Daughters of Albion* 7:8–11]

Freud connects masturbation with the autoerotic activities of
early childhood. This very connection makes these "substitutive
measures" of sexual satisfaction "by no means harmless." They
predispose individuals to "the numerous forms of neurosis and
psychosis which are conditional on a regression of the sexual life
to its infantile form."[11] There is, then, this one difference between Blake's and Freud's views of the harmfulness of masturbation: Blake's infant will be harmfully autoerotic only under the
pressure of suppression. The potential condition of infancy for
Blake is primarily characterized as "open, honest, seeking," and
it turns to solipsism through the force of culture. This formulation inverts Freud's, according to which the infant is naturally
self-centered, and opens to others through the force of culture
in the family situation. That difference between their theories is
important, as I shall show, but for both theorizers, the great
danger of masturbation is in substitute gratification. Neither
man viewed the activity as morally wrong or physiologically debilitating in the conventional way. Freud often sounds far more
like Blake on the subject, even though he connected masturba-

tion with infantile regressions, which Blake never did. Masturbation "shows the way to attain important aims in an otiose manner, instead of by energetic effort."[12]

I discuss the similarity of Blake's and Freud's conclusions about the harmfulness of masturbation because the correspondence is illuminating as an introduction to a far more significant topic. Their views on the vicissitudes of male and female sexual development under the pressure of acculturation are, as I have tried to demonstrate, essentially the same. Under the strictures of established religious morality, sexual maturation is regressive rather than progressive, and consists, according to both theories, of a series of identifications and displacements that effectively inhibit all but the most nominal degree of human happiness. "All these unavoidable and unintended consequences of the insistence upon abstinence unite in one general result: they strike at the roots of the condition of preparation for marriage, which according to the intentions of civilized sexual morality should after all be the sole heir of all sexual tendencies."[13] That "should" is not Freud's, it is important to note. The directive is issued by a moral code Freud does not approve, and his conviction is that reform is imperative. Blake felt the same way and for the same reasons, for their etiologies of sexual neurosis are nearly identical. But examination of their respective solutions to the problem compels the conclusion that each would find the other's solution horrifying and unrealistic. The seemingly minor difference in their views on masturbation contains the basis of major theoretical disagreements when they progress from cultural analysis to prophetic prescription.

It will be remembered that of the three cultural stages Freud identified, he believed contemporary morality corresponded to the third, in which "only *legitimate* procreation is allowed as a sexual aim." It is the second stage that Freud claims as a desirable "norm," by which he means "ideal fiction." In the second stage, "the whole of the sexual impulse is suppressed except that portion which subserves procreation."[14] Freud's positively phrased arguments for reform are always somewhat fuzzy and impressionistic. He is more likely to phrase his advocacy for reform in terms of protests against established mores. But on the occasions when he does edge toward direct statements, the second stage of culture is regularly invoked as a reasonable compromise reform.

Freud's reluctance to specify the changes he advocated may have been a strategy arising from his sense that the program would seem unacceptably radical to an already outraged public. If we fill in the gaps, the picture that emerges is simply this: Freud approved of sexual activity before and outside of marriage, and probably for both sexes. He never speculated in print (to my knowledge) on the way a society that permitted such activities would work, but he must have known that such changes would mean severe modifications of every imaginable kind, for they would alter the foundations of civilization—foundations whose significance Freud himself formulated.

There is in Freud's carefully phrased recommendations for reform an intentionally subversive attitude toward the entire structure of civilization. Freud whispered his manifesto for what would amount to a revolution because he dared not shout it, perhaps not even to himself. Something had to be done, he was convinced, to ease sexual tension, or civilization would eventually be crushed under its self-imposed weight. But when he asked himself what, in fact, could be done, he realized that any modification that would be strong enough to do any good would also be strong enough to alter virtually every aspect of human life. As strongly as Freud was committed to change, he also feared it deeply, because he knew that any radical alteration in sexual mores would eventually create an evolution of consciousness, with unpredictable results.

Freud could hardly recommend free sexual expression as a solution to society's ills. He needed to retain the sense of responsibility, and not just a responsibility toward human happiness. The latter would mean that sexuality would be accountable only to the pleasure principle, which is not a legitimate cultural aim by any civilized standard, least of all Freud's own. Freud never made birth control an issue in his writings, and there is no substantive evidence to suggest that he thought sexual pleasure should be recognized as its own end alone. His was still a world in which the responsible citizen must consider preservation of the species. The goal of procreation provided Freud with a rationale for sexual reform that would still be culturally acceptable, even if minimally. And Freud was not only concerned that his "ideal" should take cultural aims into account; he regarded the prospect of really free sexual expression with a horror that was entirely justified by his perspective on the essentially selfish and base nature of unfettered sexual instinct. Because procreation was the only aim Freud could envision to allow legitimate expression of the pleasure principle, his comparatively radical program for cultural transformation retained a deterministic and conservative base.

The individual at the third stage of culture is likely, thought Freud, to become either neurotic or perverted. ("Neuroses are the negative of perversions.")[15] Only a few people will approach a functional goal, for the path to it is constricted and narrow. But in the second stage, "part of the ... sexual excitation is checked, as being useless for the reproductive function, and in favorable cases is diverted to sublimation."[16] This process ends in what Freud elsewhere called "the primacy of the genital zone." But that familiar quotation is in fact incomplete without its final phrase, "in the service of the reproductive function."[17]

In a very late essay ("Female Sexuality," 1931) Freud recapitulates his late formulations on the course of this development in women, for whom the situation is "complicated by the task of renouncing that genital zone which was originally the principal one, namely, the clitoris, in favor of a new zone—the vagina."[18] This notorious statement is, I think, more descriptive than prescriptive, in that this progression is necessary to the development of "normal femininity" as our culture defines it. The element of prescription is present, but it applies to the legitimate functions of sexuality in mature life, and functions correspond to body zones. More than incidentally, that element of prescription applies to males as much as to females.

If we need further evidence that Freud actually disapproved

of sexual expression that was not oriented toward reproduction as well as (not instead of) libidinal release, his views on oral sex and other "perverse forms of intercourse between the sexes" are the final word.

> The severe standard demanded by civilization and the arduous task of abstinence have combined to make avoidance of the genital union of the sexes the main point of abstinence, whilst favoring other forms of sexual activity . . . in which other parts of the body assume the role of genitalia. . . . These activities, however, cannot be regarded as so harmless as irregularities of a similar kind interwoven with a normal love-intercourse: ethically they are reprehensible, for they degrade the love relationship of two human beings from being a serious matter to an otiose diversion, attended neither by risk nor by spiritual participation.[19]

I regard this as a particularly remarkable passage for Freud. His attitude toward oral and anal sexuality, or extragenital sexuality of any kind when not united with regular intercourse, is the same as his attitude toward masturbation. His use of the word "perverse" is not a judgmental one, it should be noted; he always uses the word in a clinical context, as a deviation from the norm in a direction opposite from neurosis. He explicitly stated that it is "inappropriate" to use the word "as a term of reproach."[20] In fact, Freud is generally very careful not to use judgmental language to describe any kind of sexual activity (as opposed to sexual abstinence), for he regards moral censure as unproductive and unscientific. It is remarkable, then, that he calls nongenital sexual activity in adults "ethically reprehensible" and "degrading." Responsible sexual expression is a "serious matter" for Freud, one that should be attended by "risks" as well as "spiritual participation." The risk is needed as a curb to unrestricted indulgence, and as a justification for restricted indulgence.

The irony inherent in his statements on legitimate outlets for adult sexuality is easy to miss, but it is one of the subtlest and most pervasive paradoxes in Freud's psychoanalytic theory. He was under unremitting attack for elevating the significance of sexuality in human behavior and personality. He protested the accusations of his critics on two basic grounds: first, they simply refused to examine the data and see that he was right; and second, they defined sexuality so narrowly that, by their definition, Freud's theories necessarily appeared absurd. Sexuality, said Freud, is the foundation of culture and consciousness, "only one must conceive of the sexual function in its true range." His own theories are conclusive evidence of the broad range he accorded it, although it should be added that he guarded against broadening it out of existence as a useful and specific term.[21] In short, Freud's conception of sexuality was not merely genital, but involved the whole body and the whole mind as well. "Psychoanalysis stands or falls," he wrote, "by the recognition of the sexual component-impulses, of the erotogenic zones, and by the consequent expansion of the idea of the 'sexual function' as opposed to the narrower one of a 'genital function.'"[22]

Yet the desirable outcome of sexual development in second-stage culture narrows sexuality back into the genitalia, literally as well as figuratively. Infancy is for Freud the only proper phase for whole-body sexuality, which must be renounced for the sake of health in the maturation sequence. In that sequence, sexuality passes from autoeroticism to object relations. In order for healthy object relations to occur, Freud thought, the diffused sexual energy of infantilism must be abandoned in favor of intense concentration in one direction. In a footnote added to the 1915 edition of his seminal essay "Infantile Sexuality," Freud ascribed the quality of "erotogenicity" to "all parts of the body and to all internal organs."[23] He never explained why he thought erotogenicity should not be retained by all parts of the body in an ideal sexual development—why, in other words, object relations could not evolve effectively without the eventual and progressive restriction of all parts of the body save the genitalia. He merely asserted that autoeroticism, if continued, would prevent successful object relating.

"The retardation of sexual development and sexual activity at which our education and culture aim is certainly not injurious to begin with."[24] This is Blake's point of departure from Freud. Blake would see Freud's ideal of free sexual expression for purposes of procreation as a useless halfway measure. The retarda-

tion of sexuality *is* injurious to begin with, in Blake's ideal, and
no amount of loosened tether after early repression will make
substantive difference. In this respect, Blake was more Freudian
than Freud. The infant "murdered" in its cradle will never behold "the arrows of the day."

Blake's own solution was expressed numerous times throughout his career, in language that remained almost identical
throughout several decades, from its first expression in *Visions of
the Daughters of Albion* to its final expression in *Jerusalem.* It consists of a fantasy of free love so radical that it still sounds peculiarly shocking in our own time.

> But silken nets and traps of adamant will Oothoon spread,
> And catch for thee girls of mild silver, or of furious gold;
> I'll lie beside thee on a bank & view their wanton play
> In lovely copulation bliss on bliss with Theotormon:
> Red as the rosy morning, lustful as the first born beam,
> Oothoon shall view his dear delight, nor e'er with jealous
>   cloud
> Come in the heaven of generous love; nor selfish blightings
>   bring.
>
> Arise you little glancing wings, and sing your infant joy!
> Arise and drink your bliss, for every thing that lives is holy!
>   [*Visions of the Daughters of Albion* 7:23-29; 8:9-10]

"Infant" means newborn, fresh, and unadulterated in a generally symbolic way, but it also refers literally to human infancy,
Blake's prototype of innocent passion. Blake's ideal expands
rather than contracts or displaces the erotogenicity of infancy.
Restriction of sexuality to the genitalia is a tyranny for Blake,
part of the whole process of contraction of possibility, through
which man closes himself up until he sees only through "narrow
chinks in his cavern." Exclusively genital sexuality is hidden and
covert, a "high priest entering by a secret place." It is only
through expansion that sex and imagination unite as functions
of human creativity, and only through that unity that love and
lovemaking become fully human acts.

One of Blake's profoundest objections to exclusive genitality is that it binds lovemaking to a reproductive model and becomes another deterministic trap. People must pass through the phase of "generation"—the boy should not "forget to generate"—but generativity in the natural sense means only endless duplication. The generativity of two people in a love relationship should be imaginative, not mimetic. In Freud, sexual energy must be sublimated in order to produce art, or any other of the "higher" cultural achievements; that is, it must be diverted, or aim-inhibited. But for Blake, art and love do not take opposite directions, and libidinal energy need not be forced into cultural aims. If permitted to develop freely, libidinal energy and creative energy will take identical form.

Blake's ideal corresponds to Freud's description of the first cultural stage, in which "the sexual impulse may be freely exercised in regard to aims which do not lead to procreation,"[25] and in which the whole body is involved in the act of loving. "Aims which do not lead to procreation" are pleasure-principle aims. "Every thing that lives is holy." Blake transforms the meaning of "holy" from set aside, secret, hidden, mysterious, to its contrary: open, free, and fully disclosed. Holiness pertains to the whole in Blake, not to a sanctioned part, whether that part is the penis in relation to the body or the priest in relation to the people. "Set apart" is replaced by "included." In the sexual fantasy, Oothoon watching Theotormon making love with other women is not voyeuristic, for her love is participative rather than possessive.

The profoundly different solutions offered by Blake and Freud to a situation they read so similarly are rooted in their basic views of the relationship between cultural aim and sexual instinct; in other words, in their attitudes toward the sublimation process. For Freud, the "intellectual processes" are classified as "displacements," so even the energy "for the work of thought itself must be supplied from sublimated erotic sources."[26] (See Chapter 2.) In terms of cultural values, the transformation is from negative (irrational, erotic) to positive (rational, nonerotic). The "grandest culture achievements" can be "brought to birth by ever greater sublimation of the components of the sexual instinct. For what motive would induce man to put his sexual energy to other uses if by any disposal of it he could obtain fully satisfying pleasure? He would never let go of this pleasure and would make no further progress."[27]

This is why Freud could not recommend anything near to unrestricted sexual freedom. The sexual instinct is naturally selfish and aggressive, and civilization could not occur without sublimation. Culture has no use for eroticism except for procreative purposes; in that sense and only in that sense is the basis of culture erotic. Sexuality in the service of the pleasure principle is a luxury Freud thought culture could not afford without severe qualifications, since culture needs a huge input of nonprocreative libidinal energy for the all-important work of sublimation. Freud thought that even if intellect was originally derived from sexual energy, an "irreconcilable antagonism" exists between them.[28]

Blake reverses the causal relationship. We are sexual beings and live our lives, think our thoughts, in a sexual context. But intellectual energy was not originally sexual; sexual energy was originally intellective. "The Treasures of Heaven are not Negations of Passion but Realities of Intellect from which All the Passions Emanate Uncurbed in their Eternal Glory."[29] Blake does not minimize the significance of sexuality with this formulation, nor does he make it antagonistic to the intellect. He inverts the progression and derivation. It is not through repression, diversion, or displacement that sex may be brought to the service of the intellect, and thereby to the service of cultural achievement. Rather, it is through these psychic processes that sexuality is perverted into forms that annihilate intellect. The pressure of culture artificially separates the sexual and the intellectual. Freud thought that left to itself, sexual energy would not transform. Blake thought that only if left to itself could sexual energy build genuinely human cities and create fully realized relationships.

5. Psychic Organization and Sexual Dialectic in Blake's *Milton*

Satan Comes to the Gates of Hell, illustration by William Blake for Milton's *Paradis*
(1808). Watercolor. Henry E. Huntington Library and Art Gallery,
San Marino, California.

Blake's major prophecies, *The Four Zoas, Milton,* and *Jerusalem,* are poetic myths that tell and retell the story of mankind's creation, fall, and redemption, and the readings they invite are as theological as they are poetic. As vehicles for Blake's systemic thought, they yield to various extraliterary emphases: political, historical, artistic, philosophical, and, in this case, psychological.[1] The assumption of my reading of Blake thus far is that psychology, and most particularly psychoanalysis, is a comprehensive category of discourse and a subsuming rubric; I acknowledge that assumption, and with it my polemical bias. I have read Blake's early works in extended analogy with Freudian psychoanalytic tenets, and I continue that general program in this reading of *Milton* as a vehicle for Blake's theories of psychic organization and sexual dialectic. Any of the three major prophecies would provide the material for similar, though not identical, readings of Blakean psychology; of the three, *Milton* is the most accessible, and requires the least discussion of Blake's mythic theology in order to be comprehensible. Together with *The Four Zoas* and *Jerusalem, Milton* constitutes Blake's version of Freud's *Totem and Taboo, Beyond the Pleasure Principle, Civilization and Its Discontents,* and *Moses and Monotheism.* These relatively late and most openly speculative Freudian texts, like Blake's major prophecies, attempt a reconstruction of psychic evolution. As we have seen in the case of *Civilization and Its Discontents,* Freud occasionally gave expression to deep regret that psychic patterns evolved as they apparently did. Blake expressed regret as deep as Freud's, based on a vision as dark as Freud's, but Blake also spoke in the prophetic and prescriptive voice Freud denied himself.

In the case of Blake's earlier and briefer works, I was able to structure pointed, detailed analogies of Blakean and Freudian psychic theory without, I think, turning Blake into Freud or forcing an alien structure on the poetic texts. It is possible to employ the same methodology with the major prophecies, but such readings, whatever their advantages, are more likely to be guilty of reductionism in the form of exacting one-to-one correspondences between Freudian concepts and Blakean characters. The result may be satisfyingly schematic, but may lose in validity what it appears to gain in precision.[2] I shall endeavor to minimize the potential for reductionist polemics here by modifying my methodology. This reading of Blake's theories of psychic organization and sexual dialectics in *Milton* will emphasize Blake's own terminology for psychic processes that are adumbrated in Freudian terms in the previous sections of this study.

In *Paradise Lost,* the battle between the forces of good and evil is the macrocosmic backdrop against which the human drama in the garden is played out. For Blake, the human drama is the macrocosm that subsumes the divine cosmology. It *is* the divine cosmology. Dramatic movement in *Milton* takes place in interior psychic space. Blake describes Milton's poetic redemption by entering Milton's mind, itself a part of what Blake called the universal humanity. The movement is reciprocal, for Milton inhabits Blake as well. Blake undertakes to save the historical and symbolic Milton from his errors, which are the major errors of culture as Blake perceived them. By employing Milton as a condensation of the Western psyche, much as he employed Albion in the later *Jerusalem* epic, Blake was able to portray through one character his version of the evolution of psychic processes, as well as his idea of the form those processes might have assumed, and should still assume.

According to Blake, Milton (for whom, as well, read "man") misperceived the relationships between reason and imagination, male and female, good and evil, God and man. In each case, Milton treated "contraries" as "negations," absolute dualities of which he could choose only one, always the "wrong" one in

Blake's view. Milton deified the reasoning process. He chose the male as model for humanity and godhead. He allied himself with "good" against "evil," which in Blake's analysis means he opted for passivity against activity, Finally, though Milton humanized Christ, his separation of God and man was absolute. He chose for God and against man, in Blake's view, however different his intentions may have been. In psychoanalytic terms, Milton always opted for the reality principle against, instead of with, the pleasure principle. He was detached from his own libidinal drives and primary process; "in fetters" when he wrote of God, and "at liberty" only when he characterized Satan.

Even a superficial consideration of Milton's complex theology and poetry will make these views sound not only simplistic but downright unfair to Milton. Milton the poet can hardly be said to oppose imagination. His values for the feminine were in many respects revolutionary. His program for pursuit of the good was not passive, requiring as it did the active participation of mankind's free will. And it can be ably argued that few theists had a higher conception of mankind's participation in godhead than did Milton. It is partly my own phrasing of Blake's ideas about Milton that makes them sound reductive and unfair, as any preliminary formulation is bound to do. Yet, finally, I am not misrepresenting Blake's analysis, because he styled his convictions in deliberately exaggerated terms. For instance, although Milton's muse in *Paradise Lost* is carefully Christianized, Blake's Milton grows to an awareness that he stands before judgment "with the daughters of memory, and not with the daughters of inspiration," that is, with the Greek mimetic muses instead of the Hebrew inspirational muses. As the epic opens, Milton is "unhappy tho in heav'n," a contradiction in terms in Milton's theology, but not in Blake's.

Patterning his song after Milton's own, Blake employs the invocation to declare his main theme for the epic. "Say first! what mov'd Milton . . . Viewing his Sixfold Emanation scatter'd thro' the deep / In torment! To go into the deep her to redeem and himself perish?" (2:16–20). The subject seems peculiar in comparison with the familiar themes Milton adumbrated, but for Blake, the relationship of poet to muse, man to woman, humanity to emanation, includes all the issues that appear on the surface to be of greater significance. The totality of psychic and epic action in *Milton* is represented in Milton's realization that even in eternity, he is separated from his emanation, Ololon. He returns to earth, to the world of experience and generation, to "put off Selfhood" and reunite with his feminine portion. The historical Milton was content first to "justify the ways of God to man," and then to "sing / recover'd Paradise to all mankind," but Blake's Milton redeems the ways of man to woman, and recovers Paradise to all humankind through that redemption.

Invocation

Daughters of Beulah! Muses who inspire the Poets Song
Record the journey of immortal Milton thro' your Realms
Of terror & mild moony lustre, in soft sexual delusions
Of varied beauty, to delight the wanderer and repose
His burning thirst & freezing hunger! Come into my hand
By your mild power; descending down the Nerves of my right
     arm
From out the Portals of my Brain, where by your ministry
The Eternal Great Humanity Divine. planted his Paradise....
                                                    [*Milton* 2:1–8]

Blake's invocation is a cryptic summation of the issues he will adumbrate in the poem. He calls upon the "Daughters of Inspiration," personalized Hebraic muses who dwell in Beulah, a sexualized or "married" paradise. The poet begets the creation (the poem) on the daughter-muses, who come "from out the portals of my brain," suggesting that they are an integral part of the poet. The diction suggests the participation of the entire body in the act of imaginative creation. It is in this manner that sexuality may be creative and redemptive, when not "divided from Imagination."

The motive force of this creativity is ambiguous. The "Eternal Great Humanity Divine" planted "his Paradise" in the poet's brain, but he did so "by your ministry." The daughters are not petty functionaries of the Great Humanity Divine, but are rather his "ministers" and administrators. It is perilously easy to seize upon Blake's use of "him" and "himself" to argue that his deity is as surely masculine as Milton's. But that resolution runs counter to the entire movement of the epic, which centers on the inclusion of the feminine as a primary principle in humanity and divinity.

"Humanity" is the key word in this context, for the divinity *is* eternal humanity. The Humanity causes the "Spectres of the Dead / to take sweet forms / In likeness of himself," a reference to Milton's reading of Genesis. In the case of a poet whose idea of humanity is demonstrably hierarchical, the "forms" of humanity will be ranked according to gender, and the use of the masculine pronoun will be significant and indicative. For Blake, however, the forms of humanity are masculine and feminine without explicit reference to hierarchy. (Implicit hierarchy is a matter I shall address later.) The "likeness of himself" in Blake is both male and female in "form," and "form" is body. Blake represents the "likeness of himself" in the engraved illumination for the Invocation. A male body grows from one side of a living plant, attached at the foot, and a female body grows from the other side. The male is accompanied by grain and the female by vines, which may represent the bread and wine of life.[3]

The "power" of the daughters is "mild," which may suggest comparative weakness, but in context here suggests rather the quality of benevolence. Harold Bloom writes that Blake admonishes as well as invokes his muses, "as is proper for a poem in which the hero goes into the deep to redeem his Emanation, and in which the Emanation herself must cast off all traces of the Female Will."[4] Bloom also points to the fact that the daughters' realm is one of "terror" and "delusion" and therefore not altogether trustworthy. It is also a world of "mild moony lustre." These are characteristic descriptions of Blake's Beulah, and

Bloom's suggestion is significant, for Beulah can open into Eternity or Ulro. But terror and delusion are not necessarily pejorative in Blake's language. There are constructive and destructive versions of feelings, ideas, and qualities in his lexicon, and "delusion" is one of the most frequently cited words with the double meanings that are part of what Northrop Frye calls the Blakean system of "analogues."[5] The "delusions" of Beulah may be negative when misused or misperceived—in other words, they may signify what is meant by the usual use of "delusion." Or they may be positive, specifically when brought to the use of the creative process, in which case they signify what men call delusions, which are really the realities of imagination.

The daughters inspire the song of the poet, who is identified anonymously as "the Bard." All of the conventional rhetoric of invocation is included in Blake's formulation, with one exception. Blake does not disavow his own abilities to minimize his own participation in the process here.[6] The emphasis is, instead, on the unity of daughters and poet. No transparent modesty veils the traditional pride of the poet, which must pretend that though the subject is worthy, he is not. Reciprocally, Blake does not elevate his muse to an abstraction that is ultimately not human. The muses inhabit his body to the point of identification. Ultimately, the daughters are his own body, and Blake is himself the bard.[7]

Emanation

Milton's "unexampled deed" is his journey to redeem his "Sixfold Emanation scatter'd thro' the deep / In torment!" (2:19–20). Milton's emanation is, on the historical-personal level, his three wives and three daughters; on the poetic level, it may refer to his works. In general, the emanation in Blake's works is the feminine aspect of any and all humanity. The female counterparts of Blake's giant "zoas" are always signified as emanations; and named emanations, with one exception, are always feminine. The first appearance of the word occurs in *The Four Zoas*, the uninscribed manuscript poem that served as quarry for *Milton* and *Jerusalem*. Prior to *The Four Zoas*, female characters and counterparts are named but not generalized. In Tharmas's first lament for Enion, the word "Emanations" appears without definition or explanation. "Lost! Lost! Lost! are my Emanations Enion O Enion . . ." (*Four Zoas* 1:18). From that time forward, Blake's use of the word to refer to female characters is consistent until the final plates of *Jerusalem*, in which one masculine emanation is mentioned.

"Emanation" was certainly a more common word in Blake's time than in ours. *The Oxford English Dictionary* cites it as "the process of flowing forth, issuing, or proceeding from anything as a source." It was "often applied to the origination of created beings from God." As an act, emanation is "emitting, evolving, producing." The *OED* cites Edward Young's *Night Thoughts* on this meaning: "The Dread Sire, on emanation bent, . . . call'd forth creation." As a noun, emanation is "that which emanates," something "emitted or radiated," especially a ray of light. Applied to immaterial things, emanation may refer to "moral and spiritual powers, virtues, qualities." Finally, it may also mean a person or thing "produced by emanation from the Divine Essence."[8] Blake began illustrating Young's *Night Thoughts* in 1796, at the same time he was working on *The Four Zoas*. It was also about this time that Blake's works were evolving into what his interpreters call a system. In the Lambeth books, which preceded *The Four Zoas*, and especially in *The Four Zoas*, the masculine–feminine dialectic had acquired sufficient metaphorical resonance to represent his convictions on art and life. It is a reasonable conjecture that Blake appropriated the word "emanation" from his work with Young. At the very least, it is certain he began to use the word contemporaneously with his illustration of Young's text.

"Emanation" is both a product and a process word, one with a high degree of flexibility and mobility of meaning. It can signify something as trivial as a branch growing from a stem or as comprehensive as the created world. By attaching it specifically to females and feminine principles, Blake manipulated all of the theological and philosophical implications of the word, extending it to its linguistic and conceptual limits. It is the theological meaning of the word that best applies to Blake's use of it throughout the major prophecies. Blake's convictions about the nature of creation and the characteristics of the generated world make it an especially appropriate vehicle to express his values for the feminine.

Blake regarded creation as fall, for it consisted of a division of wholeness into dualities and generated a synapse between eternity and time. Or rather, Blake used the concept of creation to express what he saw as the fundamental tendency toward division, schism, and dichotomy. The created world is characterized by dualities—dark and light, earth and water, male and female—and from these dualities man derived such abstractions and moral qualities as good and evil. The Eternal Humanity Divine is neither male nor female—nor even, finally, androgynous. The Humanity is not sexual at all, if by sexual is meant genital. It is only through creation that male and female are separated and *therefore* existent at all. But though creation is fall, it is also a mercy through which man may regain eternity and wholeness. If man and woman pass through the world of generated mortality, and if they continue to retain eternity through body and mind, they pass back into eternity not just at death, but in the process of daily living. This world, however, is not typically characterized by harmony, creative tension, and progression, but by greed, selfishness, war, discord, negation, and regression. It is especially in the relationship between the sexes that Blake found this lack of harmony, and especially through that relationship that Blake envisioned salvation.

The theological meanings of emanation allowed Blake to reverberate the themes that were becoming crucially important to his own theology. The emanation of a humanity (the Divine Humanity in its total form as God, or any particular humanity that is a member of the Divine Humanity) is the moral and spiritual power that radiates from it. As process, emanation is the flowing forth of inspiration. As person, it is for Blake the feminine product of evolution from eternity into generation. The entire created world, in both its positive and its negative aspects, is feminine in form. The created world was originally within the humanity, and emanated outward in the process of creation. Emanation is a derivative function, and as such might be viewed as inferior to the humanity from which it is generated; but while the emanation is not the humanity, it is the existent form of essence and the ability to mobilize energy. It is the process of creation and creation itself. Applied to the material and mortal world, Blake's connotations for emanation are ambivalent. But applied to the spiritual analogue of imagination, which is for Blake the higher reality, the connotations of emanation are redemptive.

This explanation of Blake's use of emanation, its source in his work, and its eventual identification with women in the generated world accounts for a great deal in Blake's portrayal of women and the feminine which we might otherwise find difficult to analyze without labeling Blake hypocritical or hopelessly confused. Blake was convinced that all of creation resided properly within the human form, and that history is the successive separation of humankind from itself. The separated portions of humanity become the outer world, resulting in the dualities of subject and object. The relationship between the sexes is paradigmatic for duality, since man regards woman as a projection of what is within, and treats her as another object in the object world. The fact that men have always identified nature as feminine is partly the product of this process, as Blake knew. That did not prevent him from adopting the same stance toward nature, for strategic reasons. A close reading of the action of *Milton* clarifies the development of Blake's portrayal of psychic organization and sexual dialectics, which are for him not only interrelated but identical.

Milton begins with a compressed recapitulation of the fall from Eternity. The powers of humanity in Blake's mythology are balanced in Eternity, the ideal state, in fourfold formation. Urizen is the intellect, which in fall becomes reason. Urthona is imagination, which in fall becomes Los, the "Poetic Genius" who "kept the Divine Vision in a time of trouble." Tharmas, the body of humanity in Eternity, becomes the physical body and the senses in fall, while Luvah, or passion, falls into sexual love. (It is tempting to designate exact correspondences between the four zoas in fallen form and Freud's tripartite structure of the psyche in id, ego, and superego. Urizen is certainly a fair copy of superego characteristics. Freud's ego is "first and foremost a body-ego," and Tharmas's dilemmas in the prophecies correspond sometimes very neatly to the position of the Freudian ego, which owes service to many masters. And more than fortuitous alliteration connects libido and id impulses to Luvah. But such designations, while not actually false, have such limited usefulness that to pursue them further would be to produce a schematic grid.) The cause of fall is variously described by Blake as the attempt on the part of one power to dominate the rest, creating an imbalance and a division.

Los, the "eternal prophet" who retains even in fall more of the original integrity and wholeness of eternity, is confronted with fall, or division of the whole, at the beginning of *Milton*. Because fall from unity has occurred, everything that was once comprehensively internal appears externalized and disorganized. Blake's ideal state "before the fall" corresponds to Freud's categories of primary process, which are relegated to unconsciousness after the development of what we now call consciousness. According to Freud, "a thing which in consciousness makes its appearance as two contraries is often in the unconscious a united whole."[9] In individual terms, what Los confronts at the beginning of *Milton* is what every person undergoes in the process of ego formation. "One comes to learn a procedure by which . . . one can differentiate between what is internal—what belongs to the ego—and what is external—what emanates from the outer world. In this way one makes the first step towards the introduction of the reality principle which is to dominate further development."[10] In terms of the psychic evolution of the species conjectured by Freud in *Totem and Taboo,* "primitive man transferred the structural relations of his own psyche to the outer world."[11] Freud's and Blake's value judgments on the etiology of processes they analyzed so similarly are, as we have seen, very different. But even Freud's language sometimes speaks of the stage preceding normal ego differentiation with a comprehension of its beauty: "Our present ego-feeling is . . . only a shrunken residue of a much more inclusive—indeed, an all-embracing —feeling."[12] Confronted with the loss of that feeling, Blake's Los must labor to organize the physical body of Urizen. Creating form for the material world is the result of fall, but also the merciful act that will lead to reunification. Los creates body in a series of birth images, first of Urizen, then of Enitharmon, Los's own emanation.

Both births begin with a "red round Globe," but the birth of Urizen is not from within Los. It is Los's labor at his anvil that gives form to the already separated Urizen. Before the fall, both Urizen and Los were part of the same eternal humanity, Albion. Los is creating, or giving form to, a part of himself that has already been externalized. When his work is completed, Los must himself undergo a further division, for "he became what he beheld." What he beheld was the separated form of Urizen, and, perceiving that form outside himself, he becomes a divided image also.

> . . . for a red
> Round Globe sunk down from his Bosom into the Deep in
>   pangs
> He hovered over it trembling & weeping, suspended it shook
> The nether Abyss in tremblings. he wept over it, he cherish'd
>   it
> In deadly sickening pain: till separated into a Female pale
> As the cloud that brings the snow. . . .
>
> [*Milton* 3:29-34]

The illustration in the margins of the plate shows the birth in three stages, beginning with a hairless, legless form and evolving into an almost fully developed female body. But Los is not illustrated—only the form of Enitharmon. The first birth in *Milton*, then, is a function of what appears to be a male character. Blake does not illustrate Los's labor in the engravings for *Milton*, although he did in the earlier *Book of Urizen*. In the years between the Lambeth books and *Milton*, Blake's ideas about the sexes had undergone what I regard as a major transformation, which he first expressed in Plate 4 of *Milton*, and which he maintained until the end of his life: "The Sexual is Threefold: the Human is Fourfold."

The entire concept of gender is a product of the fallen world, for gender divides. Los, unlike the other three zoas, acts predominantly for good in the fallen world, and retains more of the "divine vision" in fall. Until his further division after the creation of Urizen, Los is not precisely male. It was appropriate to illustrate Los creating Urizen in the earlier and less precise stage of his system, but not in *Milton*, where ideas regarding gender have taken on accrued symbolic significance. Though Los is "he," he is not pure male principle, but includes what will become both masculine and feminine principles in the secondary process of fall. Thus he is capable of labor not only at his anvil but in the procreative process of birthing. The "red Round Globe" is his own lifeblood separating from him, and the issue is the first generated female, Enitharmon. She is pale "as the cloud that brings the snow," foreshadowing the hard, cold, difficult relationships that will characterize men and women in recorded history. At the same time that Enitharmon is born, another birth takes place from Los.

> . . . all the while from his Back
> A blue fluid exuded in Sinews hardening in the Abyss
> Till it separated into a Male Form howling in Jealousy.
> [*Milton* 3:34–36]

The "Male Form" is Los's spectre, pure masculine principle, embodied aggression. It is the spectrous man that pursues the emanative woman in Blake's lyric poetry as well as in the prophecies. Sexuality is not essential to humanity; it is what

Blake will elsewhere call a "garment." Here he calls it "texture." Los, his emanation Enitharmon, and Los's spectre, who must be "subdued" in order to labor, build the world and generate its inhabitants. After the birth of Enitharmon, it is she that creates bodies within her body, and the sexes take on the functions history assigns them. "Her Looms vibrate with soft affections, weaving the Web of Life" (6:28). It is in earthly existence, whose place is called the "Mundane Shell," that "Men take their Sexual texture."

In the opening passages of *Milton*, Blake intends to establish a triad not of male, female, and spectre, but of fallen humanity, female, and male. "Spectre" is a term reserved for the murderous, ravaging selfhood, what Freud might have called untempered libido, or id impulse unmodified by repression and sublimation. (It is imperative to remember that for Blake, the same kind of psychic force or phenomenon develops *as the result* of mediation through repression and sublimation.) The spectre is always "insane and brutish," a creature of unrestricted and unhealthy passion, unless compelled to be otherwise. He is also the slave of reason, which for Blake is not a contradiction in terms. The spectre is the only pure "male" principle in Blake's mythology, and it is altogether negative. The positive aspect of the masculine resides in the poet, whose "aggression" is actually creative energy and activity—in this case, Los. In Freudian terms, Los and the spectre may also be regarded as embodiments of the theories of dual drives. Los embodies what Freud calls, in *Beyond the Pleasure Principle*, "the true life instincts," that is, the sexual instincts. The spectre, though it is aggressively "sexual," is the ego's repetition compulsion, the aggressive and self-destructive primal "force at work defending itself by all possible means against recovery."[13] The spectre's slavish attitude toward reason is also intelligible in Freudian terms, since what Blake called "reason" is actually not "reasonable" at all. It is like the superego, the hypermoral agency that Freud says "becomes as ruthless as only the id can be." The superego stands in contrast to the ego, "as the representative of . . . the id."[14]

The feminine principle in Blake, or emanation, is less consistently divided. Enitharmon has the potential for both good and evil, so her actions are less consistent than Los's. Los is always stronger, better, and readier than Enitharmon, who often remains recalcitrant and unpredictable, partly because she has not undergone the further division into "pure" female principle that the spectre has undergone. Blake did specify two pure female principles that operate in the fallen world: the "Shadowy Female" and the "Female Will." The Shadowy Female is the helpless, blameless urge toward incessant generativity, but the Female Will, which I shall discuss later in detail, is as self-sufficient and ruthless as the spectre. (The term "Female Will" did not evolve until much later in Blake's system, with the result that in *The Four Zoas* and *Milton*, emanations may act in the capacity of Female Will. At this stage, Blake had not separated their positive and negative functions in symbolic terminology.) The result of incomplete differentiation of females and feminine principles at this stage of Blake's mythological vocabulary is that "men" does not mean "males," nor does it mean complete humanities. Rather, it means people in the fallen and material world who are of either gender, or "sexual texture," who have the potential for complete humanity but the proclivity for destruction of self and other.

Rintrah, Palamabron, and Satan, sons of Los and Enitharmon, represent various psychic qualities and conditions. Rintrah's primary quality is wrath, Palamabron's mildness or pity, and Satan is the son who "Refuses Form." In *Milton*, Satan is no longer the active, energetic principle of *The Marriage of Heaven and Hell*. He is the prototypical spectre. The "Bard's Song" continues with the mythological incident assumed to have its source in Blake's quarrels with his patron at Felpham, Thomas Hayley. Satan attempts to take over Palamabron's functions "under pretence of pity and love." Palamabron sees Satan's ruse, "seeming a brother, being a tyrant, even thinking himself a brother / While he is murdering the just" (7:22–23). Satan takes over Palamabron's horses, and the result is chaos, for one power has usurped the place of another, creating a further fall.

Satan is out of favor and confused, and Enitharmon behaves like a mother. "She wept: she trembled! she kissed Satan. . . . She form'd a Space for Satan . . . and closed it with a tender Moon" (8:42-44). Before the Assembly of Heaven, Satan accuses Palamabron of the "Seven deadly Sins" decided upon by himself, determined by "Moral laws and cruel punishments." He declares that "I am God alone / There is no other!" His spectre, the abstraction of his selfishness, "raging furious descended into its Space" (9:25-26, 52). Once the spectre falls, Los and Enitharmon recognize that Satan is actually a form of Urizen, the god of law and reason, in generated form. The space into which the spectre descends is called Canaan, Enitharmon's world. Blake generalizes the space of Canaan into a "Female Space."

> The nature of a Female Space is this: it shrinks the Organs
> Of Life till they become Finite & Itself seems Infinite
> And Satan vibrated in the immensity of the Space.
>   [*Milton* 10:6-8]

The female space is the natural world, which man has always characterized as feminine. Blake follows the tradition in order to disclose the mysteries beneath the assumptions. Men are born of woman's womb; they come from a female space in microcosm to a larger space, the external world, to which they relate much as to the womb. They depend on it for sustenance, and they must capitulate to its laws and regulations—or they think they must. Instead of seeing the natural world as properly belonging to men, men court it, worship its powers, and call them fate, or elevate natural law to a goddess. Thus the human being becomes finite in his own eyes, and the external world seems infinite.

Satan "vibrates" in the female space because it is a world he can penetrate and suffuse, a world where men are cowed by nature and likely to "obey my principles." A male principle of aggression, war, and violent, vindictive morality gains ascendance in a world where people feel trapped within the corresponding female principle of restricted space, for which the prototype is womb. Satan is worshiped "under the Unutterable

Name," not the name of the devil but of the Old Testament God.

Leutha, "a Daughter of Beulah," appears before the Heavenly Assembly "Offering herself a Ransom for Satan, taking on her, his Sin" (11:30). "I am the Author of this Sin! by my suggestion / My parent power Satan has committed this transgression" (11:35–36). She loved Palamabron, but Palamabron's feminine aspect, Elynittria, "with her silver arrows repelled me" (11:38). The connection between the "Bard's Song" and the historical John Milton now becomes explicit. In Leutha the reader immediately recognizes Sin from *Paradise Lost,* whose "parent power" is also Satan. Leutha, in her desire for Palamabron, enters "the doors of Satan's brain night after night / Like sweet perfumes I stupified the masculine perceptions / And kept only the feminine awake. hence rose his soft / Delusory love to Palamabron" (12:4–7). She manipulated a homosexual attraction as a means to gain her heterosexual goal.

The vignette provides an explanation for Satan's ability to conquer the nations. He seemed so mild, sweet, and compassionate (all feminine qualities) that he was able to do "unkind things in kindness." Leutha separates "from the head of Satan! back the Gnomes recoil'd. / And call'd me Sin" (12:38–39). The appellation is familiar from earlier works in the Lambeth series, where the created female always shocks the eternals. As early as 1789, in his annotations to Lavater, Blake had shown similar understanding of the way men regard women in the fallen world. They say that "Womans love is Sin"—that is, it is a sin to love a woman sexually, and because women arouse desire in men, they are themselves the sin. This situation, thought Blake, described that of the historical Milton in *Paradise Lost* and *Paradise Regained.* Milton portrayed Sin as a woman, as Blake's Leutha styles herself and is styled by others, including Satan himself. What was potentially genuine affection for Palamabron on Satan's part was perverted by the misperception and misuse of qualities Blake images as feminine. It is not real love, because Leutha's qualities are Satanic when united with Satan's selfishness. What appears to be love is only "cupidity."

While Satan is the ravaging selfishness, Leutha is the genuine penitent. Blake's narrator is well disposed toward her, because she admits her transgression and hopes for redemption, much like Eve in *Paradise Lost.* Women in Blake are often more flexible than men, less hard of heart, quicker to see their mistakes and to work to redeem themselves and their counterparts, less resistant to visionary perception. Milton's Sin continues to work with Satan in his own destruction and that of mankind, but Blake's Sin is exculpated by the Divine Assembly. Implicitly, Blake introduces the idea that Milton rigidly rejected the redemptive aspect of the feminine, even though he tried to include it in *Paradise Lost.*

Leutha is brought to Palamabron after her tearful admission, and it is Palamabron's own previously jealous emanation that brings her to the tent. There she mates with Palamabron and bears Death, the "Spectre of Sleep," and Rahab, the feminine counterpart to Death. Leutha is a generating force, and fault is not the issue for Blake, as it remained for Milton. Leutha is Satan's potential creativity, which, when turned outward and misdirected, can only become perverse. Blake's illustrations for *Paradise Lost* present a related version of the characterization of woman as Sin. Differences in the two versions of "Satan Comes to the Gates of Hell" indicate a development in Blake's interpretation of Milton and a refinement in his theories of sexual psychology. In the sketchy and less finished variant, which is probably the earlier, Death is portrayed as a bearded Urizenic figure with a transparent body.[15] Satan's young and muscular body runs toward Death, and both figures advance with spears lifted, Death's toward Satan's head, Satan's toward Death's torso. Sin's pale arms and weak body push impotently against both figures. In the finished version Sin is no longer pale and insignificant. Her body, the central figure in the composition, is strong and muscular, her coils larger and more elaborate. Death's back is now to the viewer, his face young and beardless. His stance is now more defensive than aggressive, his facial expression terrified and repulsed rather than merely angry. Satan faces forward, his genitals revealed as scales, which suggest their affinity to Sin's lower body.

One final variation is easy to miss, but I regard it as the most significant. In the earlier version, Satan and Death look toward each other's heads. But in the later composition, the gaze of each is directed toward the other's genitals, and the spears likewise point toward the genitals rather than toward the head or trunk. The battle and its issues are more clearly sexual. Blake was an unusually faithful illustrator of Milton's text, as Marcia Pointon asserts.[16] Yet in this second version of Satan, Sin, and Death, Blake compromised his customary faithfulness to the details of Milton's text, which specifies that "Each at the head / Leveled his deadly aim" (*Paradise Lost* 2:711). Blake's departure from Milton's text makes the sexual emphasis of the design unambiguous and obvious. The figures of Satan, Sin, and Death are fallen aspects of one humanity, warring purposelessly against one another, and the absentee fourth figure is the unifying element of imagination. The daughter-lover in Milton, as interpreted by Blake, is the projection of the internal world to the external. The union of Satan and Sin, of sterile subject and separated object, can produce only Death, the literal "shadow" of desire and wholeness. The Gates of Hell are Blake's Ulro, where the threefold sexual vision collapses into self-divided discord and perversely ironic oneness.

The illustration is a commentary on object relations, then, but also an enactment of the incestuous violence of the family romance, which symbolizes those object relations in the psyche. I regard "Satan Comes to the Gates of Hell" as a companion piece to Plate 21 of *The First Book of Urizen,* in which Los, Orc, and Enitharmon embody an earlier stage of the same process (see Chapter 3). Both plates present father, mother, and male child. In the *Urizen* plate, the child is Orc, embodied form of revolutionary energy, who will later rise up against the father. Los perceives the child as sexual threat, and the herald of his own death. In the *Paradise Lost* illustration, Orc has grown into that embodiment of destruction which his father's perception of him compels, the spectre of life, or Death. He jealously guards the mother with whom he has coupled at the Gates of Hell, which are also her body, womb as tomb. The opponents aim where it counts, for Milton specifies that "their fatal hands / no second stroke intend." In their misguided perversion of the function of sexuality, they think, and are correct to think, that the genitals rather than the head are the place to strike the fatal blow. Misapprehension of sexuality and misuse of the body symbolize the tragic mistake of humanity, and woman's body is the battleground, which neither she nor man seems able to transform. Sin in the *Paradise Lost* illustration and Leutha in *Milton* are humanity's fatal misapprehension of "Woman's love."

As the Bard's Song in *Milton* ends, the Bard takes "refuge in Milton's bosom," and Milton rises, saying, "I go to Eternal Death!" Milton has been among the hearers of the song in Eternity, and he recognizes his own story in the tale of Satan's triumph in God's name. He has listened to the origination of the sexes and the divisions that characterize sexual relationship in poetry and in personal life, and this, too, is his story. "I in my Selfhood am that Satan: I am that Evil One! / He is my Spectre!" (14:30–31). He also realizes that he is alone "before the Judgment," without his emanation. The female presences surrounding him are "the daughters of memory," the memory of his personal failures with women as well as the spirits of mimesis. His portrayal of women and his stormy relationships with his wives and daughters have left him fragmented and unhappy in Eternity, as they did in life. "I will go down to self annihilation" means he will journey back to earth in search of his feminine counterpart, without which he lacks the ability to create, and thus to be saved. He enters the "Sea of Time and Space" as a differentiated ego.

> Then Milton knew that the Three Heavens of Beulah were beheld
> By him on earth in his bright pilgrimage of sixty years
> In those three females whom his Wives, & those three whom his Daughters

Had represented and contained, that they might be resum'd
By giving up of Selfhood: and they distant view'd his journey
In their eternal spheres, now Human, tho' their Bodies
   remain clos'd
In the dark Ulro till the judgment: also Milton knew: they and
Himself was Human, tho' now wandering thro Death's Vale
In conflict with those Female forms, which in blood and
   jealousy
Surrounded him, dividing and uniting without end or
   number.

                        [*Milton* 15:51–52; 17:1–8]

Milton could have reached the heavens of Beulah, which would
have led him to Eternity if united with his poetic genius, if he
had recognized his error. His wives and daughters represented
and contained the six females who could show him the heavens
of Beulah, a direct statement that people in the vegetated world
are symbolic, are both less and more than they appear to be. The
wives and daughters also contained the women who are, in the
Invocation, the daughters of Beulah. Their proper function as
daughters of Beulah would have been to minister to him in his
respite from the wars of Eternity, and to inspire his poetry.
Instead, he was in contention with them and cannot now redeem
himself and them without altering his thinking toward them, as
must they toward him.

   Two lines later appears a grammatical confirmation that the
completed humanity is a unified form of Milton and his wives
and daughters, or man and woman: "also Milton knew: they and
/ Himself was Human." From the eternal perspective, they are
one entity. What prevents them from being one entity is a com-
bination of Milton's Satanic selfhood and the emanations' tendency to divide and unite against him. Blake applies the activities
of dividing and uniting to emanations in all of the major
prophecies, where they divide against man and against each
other, and also unite to show their strength for working good
and evil as women in the fallen world. Women turn toward and
then away from men, continually saying come hither and go
away. The illustration for Plate 19 shows Milton's three wives

and three daughters in the top margin. The daughters dance seductively while the wives sit completely still, turning their faces and bodies away, concrete representations of dividing and uniting. Together they portray seduction and rejection, different aspects of the same action, iconographic types of Freud's narcissistic woman. At the same time that their behavior may represent the actual behavior of women toward men, and of Milton's wives and daughters toward Milton, they are also embodiments of Milton's—that is, man's—own psychic processes of projection, condensation, and displacement of internal conflict and frustration onto other people, women in particular.

For the positive form of Milton's emanations, Blake reserves the name Ololon. "There is in Eden a sweet River, of milk and liquid pearl, / Named Ololon" (21:15–16). Ololon is not precisely or exclusively a woman, or even always a feminine personage; she is the river of life from Revelation 22:1. "Then he showed me the river of the water of life, bright as crystal, flowing from the throne of God and of the Lamb." If emanation is partly defined as the total form of imaginative achievement, or "history as it should have been," then she is the aggregate form of Milton's prophetic spirit and the possibility of psychic unity. As the river of life, she is the redemptive form of nature rather than the destructive form represented by Rahab and Tirzah. Milton, Blake, and Los cannot effect further transformation without Ololon. If Milton remains alone, he will remain differentiated ego, unintegrated in Freudian terms, to say nothing of Blake's. Ololon must act in order to redeem Milton's descent into the Ulro; the emanation cannot passively await redemption. "And Ololon said, Let us descend also." She cannot save Milton in one respect, however. "You cannot renew Milton he goes to Eternal Death" (21:45–57). That is, he has volunteered to sacrifice his selfhood and to become a state of self-annihilation. Self-annihilation is not destruction of his humanity, but rather redemption of his essential humanity through destruction of his spectre. In terms Freud would understand but not agree with, self-annihation is the destruction of ego boundaries.

As Book I is the story of Milton's descent, Book II details the corresponding movement of Ololon. It begins with Blake's most extended description of the state called Beulah. Beulah is the most precarious of Blake's states of the human psyche, and its primary quality is perfect, delicate balance. Here "Contrarieties are equally true"; that is, of itself it lacks energy and tension. The characteristics of Eternity are disputive, and its primary activities are hunting and war. Beulah is the eye of the storm that rages all around it. The storms of Eternity are imaginative/poetic, and the storms of Generation are destructive. The most dangerous aspect of Beulah, that it may lead directly into Ulro, signifies that misused or misapprehended sexuality causes its participants to separate from one another, each becoming enmeshed in his or her own solipsistic subjectivity.

Beulah is maternal, "the beloved infant in his mothers bosom," and it is also highly sexual, for Blake was well aware that maternity and sexual passion are reciprocal. The daughters of Beulah minister to the "Sons of Eden" in the "moony habitation." Blake identifies the qualities of mooniness, softness, love, pity, and compassion with femininity in an entirely conventional manner. He appears to follow tradition unquestioningly. Confronted with centuries of sexual dialectics and patterns of imagery that have always defined femininity by these qualities, he is attempting to image the highest possible form or state for those qualities. He is also, even at the moments when the reader loses the connections, always addressing Milton, implicitly redressing Milton's wrongs toward femininity. Thus he speaks in Milton's own terms, which are also conventional, but often pejoratively so. Blake has made it abundantly clear that the qualities he describes as feminine or masculine are not to be equated with "humanity." They are qualities that have been attributed to the genders historically, and which males and females have perpetuated. The suffusion of such ideas into human history is so complete that however regenerative and redemptive sexuality may be, Blake became convinced there are limits beyond which sexuality cannot reach. He finally thought it best to leave the definitions as they were and to develop divine counterparts or analogues to them, but to reserve the "humanity" of each individual as a quality beyond gender.

Other considerations also determined this approach to the situation. The younger Blake planned, in such books as *The Marriage of Heaven and Hell,* to reverse the values of such Christian qualities as good and evil, God and Satan, heaven and hell. The mature Blake never shied from a challenge to approach the Bible as an adversary, but he worked from within scripture rather than from without it. He believed the Bible to be the voice of the universal poetic humanity, and it became his lifelong effort to read the Bible perversely, that is, to disclose its symbolic truths. Gradually he abandoned some of his earlier formulations. To use an example I have already discussed in another context, Satan in the major prophecies is not the hero he is in *The Marriage.* Blake undertook to disclose the real qualities of that Satan, which was simply a different way of approaching the same problem. Similarly, the reversal of connotation and denotation for good and evil was gradually abandoned because Blake was concerned to disclose the qualities of real evil and real good rather than merely to reverse their contents. "Evil" is activity and energy in *The Marriage,* but in the later prophecies Evil *is* evil.

The transformations were gradual and more than linguistic, for they entailed evolving new meanings for Blakean concepts. On the surface, Blake's use of language becomes more conservative in the major prophecies, but the appearance of conservatism is part of the process of a deeper reversal. In *Visions of the Daughters of Albion,* the feminine principle is active and energetic, precisely the reverse of conventional femininity. Blake does not abandon the idea of active-positive femininity in the prophecies, but he does make an implicit decision to retain the conventional connotations of femininity and masculinity, in order to disclose their contents and redeem their values.

The prophecies are readings of history as well as visions of Eternity, and Blake recognized that one aspect of femininity in history is softness, compassion, and tenderness. His recognition and portrayal of the latent content of those qualities (which may be precisely their opposites) are an even deeper reading of psychology. Since "masculine" and "feminine" are terms of activity and passivity historically, and since those concepts have evolved from the behavior patterns of men and women, Blake evolved in his own system both ameliorative and pejorative versions of each quality. His characterization of Beulah is thus a concretion of the positive-feminine. Thus the creation of Beulah is told in entirely conventional language regarding masculine and feminine.

> But the Emanations trembled exceedingly, nor could they
> Live, because the life of Man was too exceeding unbounded
> His joy became terrible to them, they trembled & wept
> Crying with one voice. Give us a habitation & a place
> In which we may be hidden under the shadow of wings
> For if we who are but for a time, & who pass away in winter
> Behold these wonders of Eternity we shall consume
> But you O our Fathers & Brothers, remain in Eternity
>   [*Milton* 30:21–28]

The emanations are granted their habitation, and "Like Women & Children were taken away as on wings / Of dovelike softness" (31:2–3). Blake's intention is not to equate emanations with female humanities, but that is obviously the effect. They are weak women who cannot sustain the sparring matches of Eternity. Blake is attempting to build a divine analogue to social behavior between men and women in the world of Generation, for Beulah is, according to my reading, a super-Generation. This and similar passages in the other major prophecies illustrate Blake's dilemma. *Milton* is the poem in which he is attempting to adumbrate a new idea, that humanity is beyond gender, but he is trapped in a language that reflects his own earlier process of symbol formation, as well as the accrued values of biblical and social diction.

He will elsewhere be far more solicitous to distinguish humanity from man, that is, from the male. But *Milton* represents a middle stage in Blake's process of evolution, and at this stage he apparently saw no contradiction in first insisting that humanity

and male are not the same, and then expressing the relationships between humanity and emanation as relationships between
male and female, masculine and feminine, in entirely conventional ways. In fact, if one follows Blake's own rule unbudgingly,
there may in fact be no contradiction. If gender is clothing, or
ancillary to humanity in its essence, then the characterization of
eternity and Beulah as active-masculine and passive-feminine is
not contradictory. It is perhaps the only way the relationships of
eternity can be expressed in the fallen world, since humanity is
divided into sexes in the fallen world, and there are no words for
people without gender.

The feminine-emanative portion of each humanity will seek
protection in Beulah, but this does not mean that humanities
who were female on earth must seek refuge. Rather, the
"feminine" portion of each humanity, whether male or female,
will seek refuge, because the feminine is a passive *quality*. "But
every Man returnd & went still going forward thro' / The Bosom
of the Father in Eternity on Eternity" (31:5). Eternity is a land of
father, brother, and sons; Beulah of mother, daughters, sisters,
and children.

The potential dangers of Beulah are specified in the Divine
Voice's lament. The voice addresses a woman in whom the
reader may recognize the Israel of the covenant relationship in
Isaiah, Hosea, Jeremiah.

> When I first married you, I gave you all my whole Soul
> I thought that you would love my loves & joy in my delights
> Seeking for pleasures in my pleasures O Daughter of
>   Babylon
> Then thou wast lovely, mild & gentle. now thou art terrible
> In jealousy & unlovely in my sight, because thou hast cruelly
> Cut off my loves in fury till I have no love left for thee
> [*Milton* 33:1–6]

Christianity is the unifying principle of Blake's psychic
mythology. In Christianity Blake saw the only possible vehicle
for unification of mankind. Read aright, the Bible was a sacred
code of art that would explain history and futurity. Inevitably,

Blake borrowed much of his rhetoric and imagery for the feminine from the Bible, and to the same ends that he followed other biblical usages: to express what he thought to be eternal verities and to subvert traditional readings by radical reinterpretation. The relationship between the feminine and the human (which is not the same as that between the feminine and the masculine or the male and the female) is modeled after the covenant between God and Israel. The major prophecies are courtship narratives that begin with unity, regress through separation and division, and seek reinstitution of the marriage vows—but with significant changes in the nature of those vows.

In the prophets it is always and only Israel that breaks the covenant. She is bound to love, fidelity, and trust. She breaks all three, and all three are represented by sexual fidelity. Israel plays harlot with the neighboring nations, and God treats her like the whore she has become. But Blake does not smile on that God; he is the Old Nobodaddy of the earlier books and poems, and the love he shows Israel is only law. Blake has already established his conviction that man (in this case Milton) has been as much at fault as woman in their failed marriage. In Book 2 of *Milton,* Blake intended to show the positive feminine *and* the negative feminine. The first description of Beulah shows the positive, and the lament of the Divine Voice in the songs of Beulah adumbrates the negative-feminine:

> When the Sixfold Female perceives that Milton annihilates
> Himself: that seeing all his loves by her cut off: he leaves
> Her also: intirely abstracting himself from Female loves
> She shall relent in fear of death: She shall begin to give
> Her maidens to her husband: delighting in his delight
> And then & then alone begins the happy Female joy
> As it is done in Beulah.
>
> [*Milton* 33:14-20]

This sexual fantasy is a recurring one in Blake, beginning as early as 1793 in *Visions of the Daughters of Albion.* Implicitly, the privilege of free love belongs to both sexes in the major prophecies; explicitly, it belongs to the female as well as the male in *Visions*. The subversion of scripture amounts to an almost entire reversal of content. The intent of scripture is to suggest that fidelity and love consist of exclusive possession of the sexual partner; in the prophets, God is jealous and possessive, Israel open to seduction. But the Divine Voice in Blake upbraids the woman for breaking covenant through *her* demand for exclusive possession. Reestablishing the covenant bond entails freeing the partner, not binding him. The roles are reversed, and the breach of contract is exactly the contrary. The addressee of the lament is not precisely Israel after all; it is "thou O Virgin Babylon Mother of Whoredoms" (33:20). Babylon in the Bible is hardly the virgin, but in Blake, she is the cruel and withholding virgin whose false modesty and purity engender whoredoms through repression. The sixfold female emanation of *Milton* is Babylon in her destructive and repressive aspects.

"All his loves" are not merely other women, but also the delights of life, including the imaginative joys of poetry. Through his contentions with his female dependents, Milton "abstracted himself from Female loves," that is, he turned toward reason and the classics for inspiration instead of the immediate delights of imagination, which would have been opened to him through productive relationships with women. And, Blake concludes, it must have been their fault as well as his. Affecting as it did his entire perspective on life, Milton's sexual situation determined his poetics and theology, making both rigid, formulaic, mimetic, and repressed, instead of flexible, open, inspired, and imaginative. In this respect, Blake shared Milton's own conviction that relationships with a woman concerned a man's very spiritual salvation. In these lines, Blake is reinterpreting and reprimanding the emphases of both Milton and the Bible.

The speaker of the lamentation is introduced as the "Divine Voice," who is always in Blake the Human Form Divine and Jesus, implicitly or explicitly. But at the close of the lamentation, Blake writes, "Such are the Songs of Beulah in the Lamentations of Ololon." In her eternal form, Ololon is not individual, but a

"multitude" of "Sons & Daughters." She is (or they are) the
speaker here as well as the Divine Voice, with which the multitudes of Ololon are united. The bride and Ololon are not precisely women, then, but aggregate representations of one half of
a covenant. (In *Visions*, the same message of broken marriage is
told from the point of view of the female.)

Blake carefully uses the plural pronoun "they" when referring
to Ololon in Eternity, for there she is ungenerated, not specifically of either sex. "For mighty were the multitudes of Ololon,
vast the extent / Of their great sway" (35:37–38). Within the
Ulro, Ololon sees the fallen version of themselves, the "Five
Females & the nameless Shadowy Mother," the sixfold Miltonic
female. They create Ulro, "Spinning it from their bowels with
songs of amorous delight / And melting cadences that lure the
Sleepers of Beulah down" (34:28–29). The reason females must
create the Ulro is that the conditions of Ulro are best symbolized
by the imprisoned form of the fallen body in nature, womb as
tomb. But Blake's reading of biological evolution as well as of
history recognizes that this process took place without the will of
the females in the beginning. "O piteous Female forms compelld
/ To weave the woof of death" (35:7–8).

Ololon descends through what Frye calls the "created" states,
"Southward in Milton's track."[17] She steps into the "Polypus
within the Mundane Shell," the created world of men and
women, Blake's own world. It is at this precise juncture that
Ololon becomes female.

> They could not step into Vegetable Worlds without becoming
> The enemies of Humanity except in a Female Form
> And as One Female, Ololon and all its mighty Hosts.
> Appear'd: a Virgin of twelve years. . . .
>
> [*Milton* 36:14–17]

Blake as much as says that emanations in the created world are
always female; and although he never states the case quite so
boldly, the uncreated emanations in Eternity in *Jerusalem* are
both male and female, and the created ones are always females.

The female in the fallen world is the only form of genuine, as well as false, inspiration and poetic achievement. Ololon is now a "virgin of twelve years" precisely because that is the age just before sexuality will begin to awaken. If the mistakes of history in the realm of sexual dialectics are to be retrieved, the cycle must be caught at its manifest inception. The virgin is a genuine virgin who may ripen into a repressed woman or a whore (the same thing for Blake) or take on the proper form of the emanation.

Ololon descends into Blake's own garden, and the comedy of the ensuing conversation has often been missed. Blake addresses her as "Virgin of Providence," and then asks her to support his wife, his "Shadow of delight." "Enter my Cottage, comfort her, for she is sick with fatigue" (36:32). Blake is inspired by Los, but he is still William Blake, fallen man, imperfect poet. He assumes that Ololon's mission is to support and comfort. But she is on far more important business, and she completely ignores his confused request, answering, "Knowest thou of Milton who descended / Driven from Eternity; him I seek! Terrified at my Act / In Great Eternity which thou knowest!" (37:33-35).

The "act" identifies Ololon with the Miltonic female and with the bride of the lamentation, the negative aspect of Milton's emanation. While the females in Ulro continue to divide and unite, and the bride relents, Ololon has descended to unite with those females, the bride, and Milton. Just as the negative aspect of Ololon will soon disintegrate, the negative aspect of Milton himself must undergo the same process. Milton's shadow is revealed as the "Covering Cherub & within him Satan / And Rahab" (37:8-9). The covering cherub is another form of salvation perverted to damnation, for it is the disguised form of false belief in Christian history, which "covers" the true religion and "covers" as well the intentions of the false religion of morality and justice. In order to ready himself for the ultimate remarriage with Ololon, Milton must cast off his "shadow," which is an inverted form of Satan, his spectre. Milton struggles with Satan and overcomes him, declaring that Satan teaches "Trembling &

fear, terror, constriction abject selfishness" (38:39). Milton has come to "discover before Heaven & Hell the self righteousness / In all its Hypocritic turpitude" (38:43–44). His ultimate purpose is to "cast aside from Poetry, all that is not Inspiration" (41:7). Satan is everything in him that refuses this process of purification.

Ololon watches Milton's struggle with Satan and asks, "Are those who contemn religion & seek to annihilate it / Become in their Feminine portions the causes & promoters / Of these religions?" (40:9–11). "Those who contemn religion" are the empiricists and deists of Blake's own time and other eras. Newton, Voltaire, Rousseau, and Hume are all mentioned by name. Ololon is addressing a historical irony. Attempting to free humankind from the bondage of God and "religious" morality, the spokesmen of a new world view merely raised the same God under a different banner; thus "natural religion," the worship of nature and natural forces which Blake thought forms the basis of empiricism, replaces the God of Christianity. Or, in Blake's terms, a goddess displaces a god, and the same kinds of repression and degradation of the human spirit result under a different rubric. Their "Feminine portions" are those that encourage the elevation of nature and the material world to the status of the former god; they are also symbolically those aspects of such thought which arise from passive acceptance of things as they are, a negative characteristic of the feminine throughout history. Ololon asks, "Is Ololon the cause of this?" and she is right to ask, because in the form of Milton's inspiration from the classics, nature, and mimesis, she *is* the cause.

As soon as she speaks, the answer to her question takes material form as Rahab-Babylon. Both Milton and Ololon, or more properly Milton's shadow and Ololon's Ulro incarnation, contain the delusions that Blake expresses as hermaphroditic. When Milton descended from Eternity in Book 1, he was forced to enter into his shadow in order to descend at all, just as Ololon had to take on another form, the female, in order to descend.

Milton's shadow is "a mournful form double; hermaphroditic: male & female" (14:37).

For Blake, the hermaphrodite is not the unified form of the sexes. It represents the sterile fusion of masculine and feminine in collusion against the human. The hermaphrodite is a being defined entirely in terms of genital sexuality. Each aspect hides within the confusion of mixed gender. Masculine and feminine principles, instead of enriching one another as contraries, act as negations of each other. Milton's shadow, the "Covering Cherub," hides "Female-Males, / A Male within a Female hid as in an Ark & Curtains" (37:40); that is, aggression hidden in the guise of religion, war masquerading as love or morality. The shadow contains the "Male-Females" as well, an inversion that comes out the same as its other face, "Religion hid in War, a Dragon red & hidden Harlot." Religion and morality are not good forces hidden by evil ones, but evil ones themselves, whose content is equivalent to that which hides it, or hides within its structure or form. In one, a male principle obtains power by compelling worship of external forms that are feminine and ostensibly tender. In the other, a female principle obtains power by compelling worship of external forms that are masculine and aggressive.

Milton explains to Ololon that negations must be destroyed in order for contraries to be redeemed. Negations are principles that appear opposite but are in fact the same; their relationship is static and unproductive. The true opposites may also become the same, or "identified," in Eternity, but in order for the progression to Eternity to take place, they must move through constructive tension, balance, and even conflict. "The Negation is the Spectre; the Reasoning Power in Man" (40:34). The human enslaved by reason, logic, and conservative thinking will be unable to break into the imaginative world that is the stuff of poetry and of life. Reason appears to be the antithesis of religion, but in fact, the one serves and perpetuates the other, because both are essentially conservative and repressive. Neither reason nor the external forms of religion carry the message of inspiration or freedom which may break man's fetters.

Throughout history, and especially in Milton, reason and the feminine are portrayed as antithetical. Reason is the function of the male, affection that of the female. Freud later adopted these classifications, as we shall see. Blake is, to the best of my knowledge, the first and perhaps the only reader of history and of psychological process who rejects the antithesis of masculine/ reason and feminine/emotion. He preserves the original symbolism for the terms to a great degree, and he does not reverse the formulation. Rather, he demonstrates in what manner appearances always conceal their opposites. Reason is not the antithesis of the feminine, but becomes the counterpart of the feminine, especially when both are perversely misused or misperceived. This does not mean that reason is divorced from the masculine, for the spectre is still "the Reasoning power in man," and the spectre is prototypically masculine. Since reason is not genuine intellection, Blake associates it with the negative qualities of both masculine and feminine.

When Milton summarizes all that must be cast off, "rational Demonstration" and "the rotten rags of Memory" are foremost. False creeds that arise from reason and memory must be cast off, as well as their perpetrator, the Idiot Questioner who "publishes doubt & calls it knowledge; whose Science is Despair" (41:15). (I like to preserve the fantasy that although this description fits Freud uncomfortably well, Blake might have perceived another Freud, as he perceived another Milton.) Those who perpetrate this despair are "the destroyers of Jerusalem" and the "murderers of Jesus," who "by imitation of Natures Images drawn from Remembrance" reveal this deception:

> These are the Sexual Garments, the Abomination of
>   Desolation
> Hiding the Human Lineaments as with an Ark & Curtains. . . .
>   [*Milton* 41:23–26]

This is a climactic recognition in *Milton* and the one least understood by Blake's interpreters. The "Sexual Garments" of people symbolize their genital identities, not their human identities. Genital identity finally functions to obscure human lineaments. Blake does not employ sexuality merely to *represent* division. For him, sexuality is not only the most inclusive symbol of division, but also one of its causes. With a comprehensiveness not again achieved until Freud, Blake delineated the significance of sexuality in culture. Nor was his a reductive formulation; Blake interpreted civilization as the process by which sexual energy was deflected from its aims.

The male dedication to logic and reason was for Blake a destructive channeling of sexual energy which by repressing that energy attempted to deny it. The expenditure of energy necessary to deny sexuality is all-consuming and ends in the denial of all freedom. It produces state religion, art, and science. "Negation" is Blake's word for "repression," and at the root of that repression is a ravaging lust for power, the spectre that is at bottom utterly devoid of "reasonableness." Man attempts to keep woman in his power through his claim to superior intellection, but that intellection is bloodless and cold and, in Blake's view, not "intellect" at all. Woman becomes the slave of natural religion because man's need to overpower her comes directly from his stylization of all of the forces that betray and rule him as feminine. Forced to seek a power base through subversion, woman is not only the slave of the roles man and herself have forced upon her, but also the goddess man has compelled her to be, a role she has willingly accepted. The result is what Blake later calls the Female Will, the female counterpart of the spectre. Each feeds on the other in a mutually destructive relationship that only appears to be beneficial to both. The humanity of both sexes is swallowed in the battle of the sexes, in which each negates the worth of the other.

This sounds suspiciously like a hatred of sexuality, but Blake was offering his interpretation of the way history has operated, and that operation is dismal. In fact, if culture is the expression of repressed sexual energy, then the interpreter of history who

begins with that premise is bound to present sexuality ambiva-
lently. But Blake repeated, in as many ways as his imagination
could create, the idea that it is not the expression of sexuality
that is at fault, but rather its repression. Sexuality denied—
hidden within an "Ark & Curtains"—becomes the motive power
of human life. Conceived differently, sexuality may be expressive of what Blake thought the highest in humankind—liberty,
inspiration, imaginative freedom, art. Reduced to genitality, it
infects the roots of culture like a ravaging social disease. Blake
suggests it is so pervasive that it must be purged away with Fire,
"Till Generation is swallowed up in Regeneration" (*Milton*
44:28).

Regeneration is a word Blake employed not only as a theological term but as a sexual one as well. In *The Marriage of Heaven
and Hell,* the consummation of the created world in fire "will
come to pass by an improvement of sensual enjoyment," not by
its abolition. Generation will indeed pass away, for Generation is
sexuality as it has functioned throughout history. Regeneration
transcends sexuality as we define it, illumining rather than
obscuring the human. In order for regeneration to occur, sexuality must not be a discrete characteristic of the human, but
rather such an integral part of humanity that it may be completely identical with imagination. The problem in Blake of
whether or not sexuality exists in Eternity dissolves, finally, for
the answer is both yes and no. Sexuality does not exist as we
apprehend it, as a separate function, but there is sexuality in
Blake's Eternity if by sexuality is meant full communication
among humans. Regeneration is an inclusive concept that includes Generation: "O holy Generation [Image] of regeneration!" (*Jerusalem* 7:65). Milton casts off the masculine in himself,
but casting off means integrating or appropriating, so that no
single quality will be dominant in humanity. It is the spectre's
separation from Milton's humanity that causes him to be evil.

The "Feminine Portion" of Ololon must also be cast off. "Al-
tho' our Human Power can sustain the severe contentions / Of
Friendship, our Sexual cannot" (*Milton* 41:32-33). The "virgin"

in Ololon divides from her and flees. The sexual appears to be
annihilated, but Blake has carefully chosen Ololon's age and
sexual condition. It is the "virgin" that is cast off, the incipient
but not manifest sexuality, which is the operative condition of
sexuality in the fallen world.

Blake engraves the wives and daughters once again, bathing in
the "waters of life." All six are washing off the "Not Human";
Blake engraves their body stances in direct juxtaposition to the
stances of Plate 17, where the wives remained unbudging and
the daughters danced with contorted movements. Here all are in
movement and all are touching. By bathing in the "waters of
life," they become identified with Ololon, who is the "river of
milk and pearl" in eternity.

> Then as a Moony Ark Ololon descended to Felpham's Vale
> In clouds of blood, in streams of gore, with dreadful
>   thunderings
> Into the Fires of Intellect. . . .
>
> [*Milton* 42:7–9]

The result of the casting off of sexual garments is a comprehensive defloration, in which Ololon is not the passive recip-
ient but an active participant. She is consumed and fulfilled in
the orgasmic fires of intellect, and her union is finally with Jesus.
Milton is not mentioned, for he has united with the Starry Seven
to become the Starry Eight, which in turn become Jesus. Ololon
is his "garment dipped in blood," and together they comprise
the comprehensive form of humanity, prepared "to go forth to
the Great Harvest & Vintage of the Nations."

6. Is She Also the Divine Image? Values for the Feminine in Blake

From William Blake, *For Children: The Gates of Paradise,* Plate 7 (1793).
Relief etching. Library of Congress, Rosenwald Collection.

Blake's attitudes toward sexual energy determine and are determined by his attitudes toward women. *The Gates of Paradise* provides a summary representation of what I perceive to be the problematic elements in Blake's portrayal of females and values for feminine principles. In 1793 he issued *For Children: The Gates of Paradise,* an emblem book of the fall, birth, life, death, and redemption of humanity. Although an overlay of the developed mythology that did not take form until many years later is not necessary to an understanding of this early book, all of the Blakean basics are present, including the doctrine of contraries. *The Gates of Paradise* shows the influence not only of the earlier tracts on natural religion but also of the soon-to-be articulated convictions of *The Marriage of Heaven and Hell.* Blake thought *The Gates of Paradise* continued to express his lasting concerns, as is evident from the fact that he told the same story again: twenty-five years after the original publication date he reissued the plates, emending the title from *For Children* to *For the Sexes* and adding emblematic verses, two plates of poetic "keys," and the epilogue.

The title change indicated that the same messages were operative in the worlds of innocence and experience. The emblematic nature of the book made it a compatible vehicle for Blake's ideas about sexuality over a twenty-five-year span; and yet the changes, though slight, indicate a shift in focus and emphasis. The reissue of *The Gates of Paradise* coincides with the substantive completion of the *Jerusalem* epic. If *For Children* was in some respects a counterpart to *Songs of Innocence, For the Sexes* makes the second publication an emblematic *Songs of Experience.* And as with the two sets of *Songs,* the perspective is enriched by a new emphasis on the same issues.

I take my chapter title, "Is She Also the Divine Image?" from Plate 7 of the 1818 version of *The Gates of Paradise*. In the earlier version, a young man with upraised arm engages in ambiguous action toward a tiny figure that flies upward. On the ground lies another fairy-sized human form, prostrate. The single word "Alas!" appears as caption. To use the language appropriate to this stage of Blake's development, the young man is attempting to "bind joys." In the 1818 version, however, several changes have been made, necessarily slight because Blake used the same plates. To the caption, Blake added, "What are these? . . . The Female Martyr," and below, "Is She Also the Divine Image?" The expression on the man's face in the earlier issue is one of surprised, childlike innocence. His gaze is directed upward, toward the flying figure. In the later issue his face is more mature, his expression more knowing, and his gaze directed downward.

David Erdman suggests that the young man is attempting to catch female spirits within the veil of the dead in spirit.[1] He is partly correct, for the fallen figure is clearly feminine, and in the 1818 version of the words "The Female Martyr" are printed directly below her. The figure at the upper right might be either male or female, and if one judges by comparative hair length (a fair but not infallible indicator in Blake), it is more likely male. Blake has lengthened the hair of the fallen figure slightly in the later version, perhaps as a clarification.

The "keys" to the "gates" that surround Plate 7 read as follows:

6   I rent the Veil where the Dead dwell
    When weary man enters his Cave
    He meets his Savior in the Grave
    Some find a Female Garment there
    And some a Male woven with care
    Lest the Sexual Garment sweet
    Should grow a devouring Winding sheet
7   One dies! Alas! the Living and Dead
    One is slain and One is fled
8   In Vain-glory hatcht & nurst
    By double Spectres Self Accurst. . . .

In the 1793 issue, the subject was still in emblematic form in Blake's own mind. Plate 7 may refer only to the "binding of joys," or to the trapping of the soul. The two small human figures may be male and female, or female and female. Sexual identity is not the crucial issue. But in the 1818 *For the Sexes,* sexual identity is crucial. Well before that time, the sexes had evolved into the central radical metaphor of Blake's systematic thought. It is no longer sufficient to cry "Alas!" Blake asks the central question of the place woman occupies in the Human Form Divine. The young innocent man is now the knowing man corrupted by his natural birth in the previous plate.

If the uppermost tiny figure is viewed as feminine, she may be the soul that escapes into eternity while her natural sister, the mortal body, lies dead. If that figure is male, the three form Blake's inverse trinity of fallen human, cast-out emanation, and spectrous selfhood. The "keys" suggest various possible approaches to the existence of separate sexes. The lines that accompany Plate 6 indicate that sexual identity in the natural world is both accidental and superficial, the "garment" worn by individual human forms during the sojourn in Generation. It is possible to interpret the lines accompanying Plate 7 as an inevitable assumption or absorption of the female into the male in the process of regeneration. In that case, the female is "martyred" in the sense that she loses her superficial sexual identity and becomes one with an essentially male humanity. But the unmistakably sinister tone of the engraving argues against this interpretation. Appropriation or annexation through force is not genuine unity in Blake's system; rather, it is death, or, to be more precise, murder. The preservation of "minute particulars" is as essential as its contrary, the growth toward unity.

The Gates of Paradise, like "my spectre round me" and "The Mental Traveler," is cyclic in motion and theme. The action recurs again and yet again. Spectre and emanation engage in that seemingly endless dance around the fallen humanity, and the woman old catches the child's shrieks in cups of gold. The movement of *Gates* is from before the fall—that is, before creation itself—into creation, generation, redemption, and potentially back again to the veils of the dead in spirit. Plate 1 shows the infant chrysalis and the caterpillar, both the potential butterfly of the soul and the mortal worm of the natural body. Plate 13 shows the risen spiritual body, but it is not the end of the series. Regeneration and vision may take place within the generative cycle and all around it. The traveler hastening toward his destination in the evening becomes the old man at death's door, where the cycle is completed by the cowled worm in the grave. If the reader has not taken the advice of Plate 13—"Fear & Hope are Vision"—then Plate 16, the worm, is his end. "I have said to the Worm: Thou art my mother and my sister." And the cycle can begin again: "And she found me beneath a Tree. . . ." The last lines of the "keys" leave us "Weaving to Dreams the Sexual Strife / And weeping over the web of life." The female martyr of Plate 7, interpreted as soul, is countered by the female worm of the last plate. The natural cycle is feminine, wormy, and mortal. It takes place in woman's mortal body, and returns to the tomb as womb.

These are Blake's own contraries of the feminine. Masculine and feminine, or male and female, are the sexual contraries in Blake's system, but each sex has its own negation, as we have seen. Thus, the masculine Poetic Genius is countered and foiled by the also male spectre or selfhood: Los/Milton versus Urizen/ Satan. And the feminine form of liberty or freedom is countered by the other feminine form that represents bondage to the natural cycle: Jerusalem/Ololon versus Vala/Rahab.

In *Jerusalem*, Blake attempted to adumbrate these ideas, some of which he had first articulated as dicta in *Milton*. Jerusalem's role in the epic that bears her name is analogous to Ololon's in *Milton*. Jerusalem and Ololon both become the brides of Christ, the eternal humanity. But their marriages are not duplications of earthly marriage, for the essence of earthly marriage is always exclusive possession of another person as property. "In Eternity they neither marry nor are given in marriage" (30:15). In *Jerusalem* Blake is more determined than ever to make his case:

"Humanity knows not of Sex" (44:33). At the same time, Blake's stylization of natural forces becomes increasingly sexualized.

The date on the title page of *Jerusalem* is 1808, but external and internal evidence indicate that he was revising it as late as 1818, perhaps even later.[2] During these years, Blake came to realize the limitations of his symbolic vocabulary, and attempted to make modifications that would more accurately express his convictions. He became troubled by his usage of female, male, masculine, and feminine. He had begun to use conventional meanings and to build upon them and became trapped in those usages. The emanation as feminine was now not quite what he meant. He saw emanation as light, garment, spiritual quality, creative urge and process, the liberty to imagine. That light might be "Male & Female," for if he restricted it to the feminine, he would perpetuate the distinctions of the fallen world, which he was trying to escape in his vision of eternity. The emanation, light, garment, liberty, "is Jerusalem in every Man," and Jerusalem is a "city yet a woman." His lines had been too clearly drawn, so that the concepts he attempted to purge became his masters. How can one speak of people without speaking in terms of gender? "Man is adjoined to Man by his Emanative portion: who is Jerusalem in every individual Man" (39:38-39). The emanation is actually the mediator between and among humanities in *Jerusalem*.

Blake was obviously disturbed that his language would not serve him in this most important issue, and he tried to say the same thing from various perspectives in *Jerusalem* in order to clarify the matter for himself as well as for his readers. In the fallen world, "The Feminine separates from the Masculine & both from Man, / Ceasing to be His Emanations, Life to Themselves assuming!" (90:1-2). This is perhaps his clearest and least ambiguous statement of the way things are and the way they should be. The masculine *as a quality* is as emanative as is the feminine. But the entire weight of Blake's mythology has already fixed in his reader's mind and in his own the idea that emanation is feminine and the feminine principle emanative.

Although *Jerusalem* contains the final version of Blake's vision of the proper relationship of the sexes and a modification of the identification of emanation with females, it also contains a sharp renewal of distrust toward the negative-feminine, which he finally names in *Jerusalem* as the Female Will. The Female Will is not women, but women are the manifestations of the Female Will. Female Will represents the material world, nature as destructive necessity, and the domination of forces that have been styled feminine over forces that have been styled masculine. In empiricism and "natural religion," Blake saw not the amelioration of humankind's status as sinners in the hands of an angry male god, but the subjection of humankind to natural forces that replaced that god, duplicating or even exceeding his vindictiveness, arbitrariness, and restrictiveness.

For Blake, the emergence of nature as the primary redemptive symbol of romanticism was not a reaction against the Age of Reason, but rather its fulfillment and culmination. Man had always imaged nature as feminine, and Blake perceived that process of symbol formation as one in which man grew not larger but even smaller than he was under the auspices of Christianity. Nor was the Age of Reason itself a reaction against Christian theology as enacted in culture; it was part of the same evolutionary process, one that was increasingly regressive rather than progressive. Man was no longer at the mercy of a spiritual world that was infinite, though that was dismal enough; now he was at the mercy of a material and natural world that was finite. The old religion had at least infinity to recommend it to Blake. The new dispensation appeared to open all the world to man's knowledge, but that world was smaller imaginatively—or if its expanses were granted, they were seen as beyond man's grasp in a manner finally little different from that posited by preceding world views. Man's creative energies were now consumed by his relationships with the object world, which he thought of as external to himself. In this process, Blake saw yet another aspect of the same divisiveness that had characterized other periods of history, one rooted like the others in sexual dialectics. The Female Will was his personified representation of the separateness of nature from man. Nature is things-as-they-are, not things-as-they-might-be, and if man models himself after nature, he can see himself only as finite, even minute.

Blake was so enraged by the process of nature deification in the late eighteenth and early nineteenth centuries that his historical moment accounts for his almost obsessive preoccupation with the Female Will. The Female Will is present as early as *Europe* (1794), in the acts of Enitharmon. In *Europe*, Christian history is portrayed as "a female dream," and man himself is only woman's dream.

> Now comes the night of Enitharmon's joy!
> Who shall I call? Who shall I send?
> That Woman, lovely Woman! may have dominion?
> [*Europe* 6:1–3]

It seems a curious reading of history indeed, for Blake knew very well that Christian culture was patriarchal, and demonstrated that knowledge in many poems, especially in *Visions of the Daughters of Albion,* published the previous year. Throughout his life he objected to man's repression of woman's freedom, expressed primarily through the laws of Urizen, the Old Testament Jehovah. But he saw the process as subversively reciprocal. Woman was taught that her sexuality was unclean and sinful. Therefore, she repressed it and withheld it from herself and from man. That power base, the passive-aggressive, became a comprehensive one in Blake's view. The withholding of sexuality in the name of moral virtue and Christian propriety had been woman's chief function in civilization, to her everlasting detriment and to man's. Woman used her withheld sexuality first as a protection, then as a bludgeon. "Go! Tell the Human race that Woman's love is Sin!" cries Enitharmon,

> That an Eternal life awaits the worm of sixty winters
> In an allegorical abode where existence hath never come.
> Forbid all Joy, & from her childhood shall the little female
> Spread nets in every secret path.
> [*Europe* 6:5–9]

The allegorical abode is the Christian heaven, which is to be attained by a renunciation of pleasure in this world. In the earlier works, Blake carefully balances the fault: Urizen has forced the female, who then becomes complicit in the crime against humanity.

In *Jerusalem,* Blake continues to attempt a balance of causal attribution. The male spectre is the counterpart of the Female Will, and he is meant to appear as destructive and dangerous as the Female Will. Blake made what seems every possible effort to establish that Female Will is not equivalent to woman, but that woman is the manifestation of the Female Will because she is identified with nature throughout history. As he grew older, Blake became more and more convinced that nature worship was the primary manifestation of man's fall in his own time and, correspondingly, his vehemence against it increased. He named his final epic *Jerusalem,* in honor of the redemptive form of woman as liberty, inspiration, and the process of poetry. But any accounting of Blake's values for the feminine is also obliged to come to terms with some peculiarly strong statements in *Jerusalem.*

Los, Blake's own spokesman, cries:

> What may Man be? who can tell. but what may Woman be?
> To have power over Man from Cradle to corruptive grave.
> There is a Throne in every Man, it is the Throne of God
> This Woman has claimd as her own & Man is no more.
> [*Jerusalem* 30:25–28]

Blake is speaking of man's entrapment in physical mortality and his enslavement to nature. As before, Blake's intention is to include the female in the term "man." But in *Jerusalem* it becomes increasingly difficult for Blake and his reader to feel that inclusion. In *Milton,* Blake carefully abstained from using the word "woman" to express his convictions about forces that have been portrayed as feminine. *Milton* reads like a strategic and judicious withdrawal of that term from its overuse in *Europe.* But in *Jerusalem,* woman in the fallen world is repeatedly equated with

the Female Will. "O Albion why wilt thou Create a Female Will?"
(30:31). The negative aspect of the sexual was in *Milton* more
evenly divided between the separated masculine and feminine
forms, Satan/spectre/shadow and the sixfold Miltonic female.
But in *Jerusalem* the "Sexual Machine" is predominantly female,
"an Aged Virgin Form" (39:25). "This World is all a cradle . . ."
(56:8). Increasingly, woman in fall is only natural body, only
oppressive maternity. Vala, the erring emanation in *Jerusalem*,
cries, "The Human Divine is Womans Shadow, a Vapor in the
summers heat." He is "Woman-born / And Woman-nourished &
Woman-educated & Woman-scorn'd!" (64:16–17). The torture
of humans that was accomplished by both sons and daughters of
Albion in *Milton* is almost exclusively the function of the
daughters in *Jerusalem*.

The description of Beulah is now "Where every Female delights to give her maiden to her husband / The Female searches
sea & land for gratifications to the / Male Genius" (69:15–17).
Rahab and Vala rage through the pages of *Jerusalem* with their
train of daughters and witches, destroying everything in their
path. "O who can withstand her power / Her name is Vala in
eternity: in Time her name is Rahab" (70:30–31). The intentions
of the women are total destruction of the men. Enitharmon
decides to "exhaust in War" the "fury of man" so that "Woman
permanent remain" (82:35).

Blake reminds the reader periodically that woman's alliance is,
after all, with Satan, "the God of this world," and with "the
Patriarchal pomp and cruelty," but the reminders read as inter-
ludes in a sustained tirade against nature and increasingly,
therefore, against woman. The contention of Los and Enitharmon becomes a battle of wills, for "Two Wills they had, and two
Intellects." The emanation that before seemed to be a nearly
equal partner in the united humanity is now just as often presented as the aspect that must merely capitulate; the emanation
"refusest my Fibres of dominion" (88:13). Theoretically, the
spectre must also be under the dominion of the humanity, and
in these very passages Blake is attempting to break the identifica-

tion of emanation with woman. But the emanation to whom Los speaks is Enitharmon, who is by definition a female in the fallen world. And she answers him, "This is Womans World," and declares that she will increase her power "Till God himself becomes a Male subservient to the Female" (88:21).

At the same time, *Jerusalem* also contains the most fully developed version of the positive-feminine, the redemptive form of Jerusalem. Throughout *Jerusalem,* she attempts to persuade her negative counterparts to work with her. Blake's rage is against nature, and Jerusalem is not natural but spiritual. "Vala produc'd the Bodies Jerusalem gave the Souls" (18:7). *Jerusalem* ends in the marriage of Jerusalem and Albion, and thereby with inclusion of the feminine principle in humanity. But because Blake believed that "humanity is far beyond sexual organization," he was obliged to seek human relationship other than marriage to symbolize the highest form of communication in Eternity. That relationship evolves in the major prophecies as brotherhood through Christ. "This is Friendship & Brotherhood without it Man Is Not" (96:16). Though "Sexes must vanish & cease to be" in Eternity, Blake describes the relationships of Eternity in gendered language, perhaps because our language is gender-bound and created from that sexual dialectic.

The image of woman in *Jerusalem* solidifies, then, into unfortunate extremes. In *Milton,* Ololon and the sixfold female "represented and contained" all positive and negative aspects of the feminine. In *Jerusalem,* each woman is characterized *only* by extremes: she is either Vala/Rahab or Jerusalem, ravaging destructive principle or redemptive principle. There seems far less room for "real" women here than in Blake's earlier work. That last-minute leap into Eternity—which is technically genderless —must accomplish woman's salvation, for her aspect in the fallen world in *Jerusalem* is uniformly ghastly. There were frequent indications of this development in *Milton.* "But every Man returnd & went still going forward thro' / The Bosom of the Father in Eternity on Eternity" (31:4–5) is a formulation that, whatever its intentions, reads curiously like "patriarchal pomp."

But *Milton* is without the tirades against Female Will that threaten to overpower Blake's vision of theoretical equality between sexless sexes in eternity. It would be convenient to redeem Blake's view of woman to accord with what were clearly his intentions, and to do so by emphasizing that the Female Will is not really woman at all. Blake's mythology was highly symbolic, and his symbolism might be brought to his rescue on exactly this issue. An analysis of metaphorical process in Blake, however, compounds rather than simplifies the problem.

Blake's composite portrayal of females and the feminine has been the cause of continuous confusion for his readers. Even the best of his readers seem unable to fathom the situation. Northrop Frye's "Notes for a Commentary on *Milton*" summarize what I read as a contradiction, or at least an immense difficulty, in Blake as well as in his critics. Frye details the structure of the fourfold in Blake's symbolism. In Eden or eternity, "man is one with God, and everything else is part of a divine, and therefore a human, creation."[3] In the natural world, only similarity and separation are perceived. In the imaginative or eternal view, Blake speaks of "Identities of Things."

> A thing may be identified *as* itself, yet it cannot be identified except as an individual of a class. The class is its "living form," not its abstract essence, and form in Blake is a synonym for image, or experienced reality.... All Blake's images and mythical figures are "minute particulars" or individuals identified with their total forms. Hence they are "States, Combinations of Individuals," and can be seen in other singular or collective aspects.[4]

In other words, all things are identical with each other. In the imaginative view, all things are within the human form, and all forms or images of that body are identical. Frye argues that such a vision can be expressed only through metaphor, and the metaphor, in its radical form, "is a statement of identification." Everything may be one in "essence" but infinitely varied in "identity." This is surely one of the reasons Blake turns to Christianity, whose language Frye calls "instinctively metaphorical."

Christ *is* God and man. *Revelation* expresses a world view in which all things have attained human rather than merely natural form. The divine world, then, is one in which all aspects of infinite and eternal humanity are One God. The human world, from the imaginative point of view, is one in which all men are one man, "expressed in terms of sexual rather than social love, a world in which a Bridegroom and Bride are one Flesh." In Generation, the imaginative and natural visions battle; in Beulah, "nature begins to take on its proper form of a female 'emanation' loved because created. Christianity preserves this symbolism when it speaks of the Church as the Bride of Christ."[5]

On one hand, then, Blake can be defended against accusations of hating women through his tirades against the Female Will precisely because the Female Will is not women. But the Poetic Genius is not that which finds mere similarity; it is that which creates "identification." Blake claimed the status of "vision" for his entire mythology. If women are the manifestation of the Female Will, or the destructiveness of nature, then they *are* the Female Will. The "female" is a "form" in Blake, and thus an image. Female human beings can be identified only as individuals of a class, to follow Frye's formulations. That class is "human beings of the feminine gender." This is the feminine existence, for there is only one essence, which is eternal and not sexual. Blake constantly reminded his readers that they must not mistake an "Individual" for a "State." "Distinguish therefore States from Individuals in those States" (*Jerusalem* 32:22). States are abstractions, and individuals are humanities, not abstractions. Blake always counseled that abstraction was the enemy of mankind, but in his rage at the natural world, Blake forgot his own first rule. Women in the fallen world in *Jerusalem* are not portrayed as "Minute Particulars," but as abstractions of the Female Will, utterly identified with nature. Woman is redeemed in Eternity, but not as woman. In Eternity the female humanity is an "individual identified with its total form," the Human Form Divine. But in Generation she is also identified with her total form, the form of the natural world.

The redemptive form of the feminine must be found, then, in Eternity. Frye has this to say about the nature of gender in Eternity: "In Eden there is no Mother-God. . . . God is always the Supreme Male, the creator for whom the distinction between the beloved female and created child has disappeared."[6] Despite Blake's warnings to the contrary, even so sensitive a reader as Frye has managed to miss Blake's point. But it might also be suggested that Blake missed his own point. How did this state of affairs come about?

Blake was the product of his acculturation. The fact that he could perceive and anatomize the processes of symbol formation in culture did not mean that he was immune to them himself. His representation of nature as feminine was not merely a strategy by which he adopted the historical terminology in order to destroy it or to disclose its true meaning. According to his own analysis of the development of consciousness in the fallen world, the perception of nature as feminine was deeply ingrained in his own thought processes. He was well able to see what that iden tification had produced in history, but less able, not surprisingly, to perceive the long-range results of his own appropriation of the conventional terminology which eventually restricted his capacity to portray the feminine.

In the Dante series, begun about 1824 and left unfinished at Blake's death, woman is treacherous and delusive. Blake was convinced that Dante had made "the Goddess Nature & not the Holy Ghost" the foundation of his belief.[7] Beatrice, far from being the spiritual inspiration she is in the source text, is instead portrayed as the Goddess Nature, a form of Rahab/Vala. Woman/man configurations in the heavily symbolic *Purgatorio* and *Paradiso* designs are consistently styled as Nature/man confrontations. In "Beatrice Addressing Dante from the Car," Dante gestures in submission to Beatrice, poetic genius subordinating itself to Female Will. Plate 16, "The Goddess of Fortune," portrays a Vala-like figure presiding under twin globes of materialism and rationalism.[8] Above her head, Blake wrote in pencil, "The Hole of a Shit-house. The Goddess Fortune is the

Devil's servant, ready to Kiss any one's arse." In their sketchy form, the twin globes are unmistakably a woman's breasts. The large circle in which are drawn Vala and the acerbic remarks are the ample belly and hips of the vegetative female, Nature.

Just as Blake could not stand completely outside history or consciousness, neither could he absent himself from the social arena. The pressures and tensions of sexuality were his own as well as other men's. It is improbable that he could so clearly have understood the process by which men project women as the elusive other, and spend their lives pursuing and attempting to appropriate women, unless he had been the victim of that process himself. Blake resented nature and what he called the Female Will, and he probably also resented real women as embodiments of those forces. It is not merely that history has styled those forces as feminine, but that Blake felt them as feminine also. And that feeling is partly the result of processes that are biologically determined.

We are of woman born. Our bodies die. Blake saw the idea of bodily mortality as pernicious, for it denied another and higher reality. Women are not capriciously chosen by Blake as symbols of the natural world; they are the bearers and first nurturers of humanity. Body means woman, and Blake loved the body, which, when used expansively, was a gateway into Eternity. Bodily birth and death are inevitable, and Blake was ready to make the best of it, but not to acknowledge it as the all. He was a realist who was determined to love the body for its potential, even as he hated its limitations. But he was so hypersensitively aware of the dangers of the body that his early critics may be forgiven for mistaking him as a body hater—they are wrong, but not altogether wrong. It is the natural and mortal body that Blake loved and hated, and though the potential for spiritual regeneration lies in the physical body, the actuality does not. (The actuality is in Eternity.) Blake calls the new body a "spiritual" body. To the extent that he saw the natural body as the enemy of humanity, to almost exactly that extent he saw woman as the enemy of humanity. Woman *as woman* is her own enemy and man's as well.

Man *as man* is the same. Body is a positive aspect of humanity when it is used as a gateway out of body or beyond body, in such a way as to include body.

According to his own analysis, Blake is entirely justified in adopting conventional diction to characterize "masculine" and "feminine," for he is describing the historical evolution of those "principles," and he takes care not to equate them with men and women in their human form. "Reason and Energy, Love and Hate, are necessary to Human existence. From these contraries spring what the religious call Good & Evil. Good is the passive that obeys Reason. Evil is the active springing from energy" (*The Marriage of Heaven and Hell*, Plate 3). Though reason and energy, active and passive, are contraries, and both are necessary, active energy is superior to passive reason. By following the conventional meanings of masculine and feminine, Blake associated "reasoning passivity" with the feminine and "imaginative activity" with the masculine. This does not mean that women in Blake do not act. But when they do, they are not being "feminine," but rather female. The feminine is a passive category in Blake, but the Female Will is active in the extreme. Feminine passivity may be either valuable or pernicious, as may masculine activity. But by following historical symbols and then trying to reorient them, Blake became mired in the inevitable identification of female, feminine principle, and woman.

Blake's problems with portrayals of sexuality and of women, as I see it, are problems of symbol formation that express themselves in the limitations of language. If, as Blake posits, consciousness itself is sexual, dialectic, and gender-specific, then the development of language will also be gendered; and this is, of course, the case. Blake's vision of the human form and his idea of the value of being human was constantly rendered problematic by language. He had to try to speak the literally unspeakable. Language and art were his tools for reunification of the Human Form Divine, but the images available to him to communicate his vision of the eternal were necessarily drawn from the repository of the material and natural world. That world—its images and therefore its language—was sexual. Blake wished to portray everything as human, and humans in this world are sexual beings. He was thus compelled to express ultimately genderless human forms in gendered terms.

If "Humanity Is far beyond sexual organization," then it is also beyond language and image. There are, quite literally, no words that will completely express Blake's vision. Poetry and art in the fallen world are keepers of the divine vision, but they must make do with the tools at hand. The major prophecies are Blake's use of those tools, a documentation of his effort to say everything in as many ways as possible, in the visionary hope that the whole would be recognized as more than the sum of its parts. To accomplish this task, he turned in every direction; most of all, to the sexes. Here, where he tried hardest to heal, he was constantly confronted with the wound. Sometimes, ironically, he deepened the wound.

There are, I think, other reasons Blake's prophecies move in directions that are less and less sympathetic to women in the fallen world. The major villains of the earlier works, and especially those of the 1790s, tend to be portrayed as male. The proportion of villainy that falls to the female in the later work is significantly greater. This shift is partly the product of his historical situation. In the earlier works, Blake saw the major historical movement against which he must revolt as the Age of Reason. Because abstract reasoning is a masculine principle in the evolution of culture, it is to be expected that Blake would portray it as male. But in the first decades of the 1800s, romanticism was the spirit of the age, and with romanticism came the deification of nature as goddess. As I have tried to suggest, the two movements and their sexual reflections or symbols are not antithetical for Blake; they are integral developments that grow out of one another. They are not proper contraries at all, but merely negations that duplicate themselves and cancel out any possible progress. The animating spirit of the first is masculine, and the animating spirit of the second is feminine. What appears to be (and in some respects is) a mounting vehemence toward natural

women, simultaneously developed with the regeneration of
spiritual woman, is a product of Blake's particular moment.

One further mitigating factor remains to be considered in
Blake's comprehensive portrayal of the Female Will. It accounts
in part for the way in which the Female Will dominates the
action of *Jerusalem*. Blake was better able to name and embody
the destructive forces exerted by men in history for a simple
reason: there were many more names available to him. The
qualities he damns in men can be divided among numerous
historical personages as well as among his mythical characters.
Bacon, Newton, Locke, Voltaire, Titian, Rubens, Dante, Milton:
the prophecies are full of their names. But there was no such
historical gallery open to Blake when he wished to "give a body
to Error" in the female. He was forced to make do with biblical
women and his own mythological characters. To make up for
the lack, he postulated the Female Will, a name that suffers from
abstraction and overgeneralization because her "Minute Particulars" had few familiar names in history.

Blake was able to perceive the limitations of Milton's values for
the feminine, and there is some evidence in *Jerusalem* that he was
beginning to perceive his own. That he was not able to perceive
all of them is not entirely a failure on his part. Rather, the
degree to which he valued the feminine is unprecedented. Writing a century and more after Milton, he advanced Milton's
thought on the sexes by an immeasurable degree. In apocalypse,
"the Hand of Man grasps firm between the Male & Female
Loves" (*Jerusalem* 97:15). Jerusalem disappears as an individual
character at the end of *Jerusalem* because she has at last awak-
ened and "overspread all Nations as in Ancient Time" (97:2).
City and woman, the absolute redemptive form of humanity in
her book as Milton is in *Milton*, she suffuses "All Human
Forms." Jerusalem is the "name" of all emanations, the ability to
move freely between time and space, the impulse to create, and
creation itself as living process. Blake preserved more of Milton's
"mistaken" vision than I believed he intended, but far less of it
than most of his own predecessors and successors.

Milton's idea of what constituted the proper relationship between the sexes was radical and revolutionary—and also conservative and reactionary. He attempted to change the basis of sexual interaction only to a certain degree, and the foundation, feminine inferiority, remained intact. Blake intended to abolish that inequality but, like Milton, found there were assumptions he was unwilling or perhaps unable to part with. Blake battled sexual repression in Milton and in himself. Freud continued the process a century after Blake. It is now nearly another century since Freud first began to write, and culture has not come very far since then. Whatever the limitations of Blake's vision may have been, I cannot fairly fault them. Culture, as opposed to small numbers of individuals within it, has not begun to approach Blake's vision, and it is only beginning to approach Milton's. Blake would be disappointed, but not in the least surprised.

He might be surprised, however, by the kinds of criticism to which his works are increasingly subject in the political climate of this decade. I quote at length from Susan Fox's predominantly excellent analysis, "The Female as Metaphor in William Blake's Poetry," because it illustrates an emergent tendency in Blake criticism which I find troublesome.

> Blake made the chief character of *Visions of the Daughters of Albion* female not just because he admired Mary Wollstonecraft and thought women at least potentially men's equals, but also because he needed a chief character who could be raped and tied down and suppressed without recourse—or rather, with the single recourse of giving birth to the revolutionary male force which can end the victimization. *Visions of the Daughters of Albion* has a heroine and not a hero partly because one of the points of the poem is that its central figure, "the soft soul of America," is a slave. Oothoon was chosen for her part not just because she was wise and brave, but also because she was female and thus powerless. Her gender is a trap—just the trap the symbolism of the poem demands. Blake rails against her being trapped, of course—he was never not libertarian. But it is one thing to despise oppression, and another to envision the means of the oppressed to end it. No woman in any

Blake poem has both the will and the power to initiate her own salvation—not even the strongest and most independent of his women, Oothoon.[9]

It is important to note that Fox is dealing not with the Female Will, the issue on which Blake is admittedly most open to critical remonstrance, but rather with Blake's most openly feminist poem. I appreciate Fox's motives, but her analysis suffers from the same kind of expectation that characterizes the objections of Freud's critics on the same subject: that description somehow suggests prescription, and/or that description should be succeeded by alternative prescription. The analogy with Freud's critics is more than fortuitous, because Blake's and Freud's perceptions of femininity were very similar. Several significant problems are summarized in this excerpt from Fox's essay.

First, it is indeed important that Blake wrote *Visions of the Daughters of Albion* shortly after he illustrated Wollstonecraft's book of short stories.[10] The works of the 1790s show a conscious occupation of Blake's energies with issues that might be termed feminist. The political allegory is also important for Blake during this period, during which he wrote such less disguised political treatises as *America* and *Europe*. But Fox points out the aptness of Blake's metaphorical use of females in the political allegory as much to castigate as to praise him. She appears to fault Blake for not "envisioning the means of the oppressed to end [oppression]." This judgment effectively removes *Visions* from its context in Blake's career. With the possible and only partial exception of *The Marriage of Heaven and Hell*, the early works are not intended to enact regeneration. They are readings of history as it is, not as it should have been or might be in the future. By selecting a woman to represent America in the political allegory and womanhood in the sociosexual allegory, Blake serves the first purpose of transformation by providing a penetrating analysis. Synthesis will come later, in the major prophecies. I am more sympathetic to criticisms of the ways in which Blake envisions feminine participation in "the means to end oppression" than I am to criticisms that he did not manage it at the beginning of his career. And it is only a half-truth that no woman in Blake initiates her own salvation. For the most part, neither do men, nor can one sex do so without the active cooperation of the other.

Even if *Visions* is less prophecy than history, it does indeed contain prophetic passages that envision the means to end oppression (as we have seen). People cannot escape their tyrants, according to Blake, until those tyrants are exposed. Even in the major prophecies, disclosure is more than the prelude to transformation; it is an integral part of the redemptive process. And Oothoon, a woman, is the speaker of all of the prophetic passages in *Visions*. (Fox's reading of Blake is always knowledgeable and perceptive, and often superb. Even competent readers of Blake will misread him on the feminine unless the complexities addressed here are considered.)

Blake's early characterizations of women are primarily as victims because women were, historically, victims. But for Blake, women were victimizers as well. The symbolic content of the Female Will is perhaps the major problem in Blake's characterizations of the feminine, but it is not the only one. The literal and historical levels on which real men and women interact were a large part of Blake's concern, and women are seldom faultless on those levels. I can most clearly illustrate my points by continuing the parallels between Blake and Freud.

As Juliet Mitchell has shown in *Psychoanalysis and Feminism,* those who condemn Freud for his views on women usually fail to understand that Freud's is an *analysis of* patriarchy. More fundamental still, Freud's critics often do not accept the tenets of psychoanalysis at all.[11] Mitchell's major point is that by dismissing and misjudging Freud, women discard an important ally. They identify him with the facts he discovered, and they do not like those facts; hence, they must not be facts. Freud provides us with the most comprehensive psychological dramatization of patriarchy available. If that dramatization includes some unpleasant things about what the feminine has meant, in culture and in individuals, his critics hold him responsible. This attitude precludes not only an understanding of his worth as cultural historian, but also the use of his findings in the attempt to transform culture. It also effectively precludes, in my view, the possibility of ascertaining the ways in which some of his findings really were culture-specific, and therefore of only very limited use.

I anticipate the same process in Blake criticism. In the case of earlier critiques, the process is already evident.[12] The relationship of masculine to feminine and of man to woman is perceived as the foundation of consciousness by both Blake and Freud. Accurate reading of Blake requires, as fully as does accurate reading of Freud, acceptance of the axioms of psychoanalysis: full acknowledgment of the range of unconscious thought processes and of the role of sexuality in human personality. Infantile sexuality and oedipal configurations, though they appear in considerably modified form, are also implicitly fundamental in Blake.

I do not think that most feminist critics come to Blake with a sympathetic approach to this apparatus. (Most people do not have the slightest inclination to accept the range and significance of sexuality and unconscious thought.) Blake critics, as a group, may be more likely to accept these axioms, or at least to pay them lip service. But, as Mitchell points out, many successful psychologists, and even some psychoanalysts, do not really accept these dicta. (Mitchell cites Reich as a famous example of an analyst who did not believe in the unconscious.)[13] What has happened in Freudian criticism is, I think, likely to occur in Blake scholarship, from within the circle of aficionados as well as from without. The more widely Blake is read, the more he will be misapprehended, as Freud has been. And there is every evidence that Blake's popularity is still increasing.[14] This era will be as touchily sensitive to Blake's convictions about sexuality as it is to Freud's. Earlier Blake critics tended to misread Blake on women because the subject was not, in particular, an issue for them. Contemporary Blake critics misread him on the same subject because it *is* such an issue for them, and for our time.

One final reason I think this tendency to misread Blake on women and the feminine will increase is based not on his similarity to Freud, but on a clear difference. Freud did little to suggest in what ways women might have contributed to their own denigration. Instead, he simply accepted feminine conditioning as a given imposed upon women. When he protested it, as he often did, he protested against cultural trends, not against people. The supposedly weaker sense of justice in women is attributed by Freud to the weaker foundation of the superego in women. The lack of intellectual distinction in women arises from undue and excessive suppression of the sexual instincts; hence, women have less energy available for the all-important work of sublimation.[15] Freud's critics looked only at the result he presented (in these examples, a weaker sense of justice and a lack of intellection), entirely omitting consideration of the analysis that underlies it, an analysis that admits that society *made* women weaker. It does not occur to such critics that Freud was in some respects right, and that his analysis explains rather than justifies the conditions. (He does, at some few points, attempt to justify such conditions. In either case, that is beside the point.)

Defined as patriarchal society has defined it, intellectual capacity in women, or at least its manifestation in culture, *is* historically weaker in women than in men. So, too, is the sense of "justice," for justice is subjectively masculine, Judaic, and derived from law. If such mistakes of interpretation have been so consistently made in the case of Freud, who saw women almost exclusively as victims, one might expect even greater mistakes in the case of Blake, who saw women as both victims and victimizers. Not content to leave woman nursing her other-imposed neurosis within the confines of the kitchen, Blake analyzed the ways in which women not only submitted to their own denigration but helped it along, and thereby gained power through manipulation in the passive-aggressive mode. Blake's sense of women's significance in the external events of history was also far keener than Freud's, and Blake was as hard on women as on men for the mess that history is.

The need to be free of responsibility for things-as-they-are is, I believe, a disturbing characteristic of the neo-feminist movement, one that implicitly attempts to salvage the exclusive privileges that accrue to the oppressed in a historical scenario in which women are only victims. Blake's prophetic fury fell on women as fully as on men because he did not accept the idea that women are, or ever were, only unwilling innocents. His condemnations of traditional feminine behavior, like Swift's, were rooted in the conviction that woman herself deserved far better—that what appeared to constitute virtue was in fact a profound self-betrayal.

7. Freud and Feminine Psychology

William Blake, Hecate (1795). Color print finished in watercolor and pen. The Tate Gallery, London.

Since Freud is better known and more widely accepted than Blake in the twentieth century, I have measured Blake's knowledge of the human psyche by its correspondence to Freud's. And since Freud's use of language and patterns of perception are more accessible to the contemporary reader, I have attempted to make the mythopoesis of Blake intelligible in Freudian terms: "Like Freud, Blake . . . " I reverse my methodology here and adumbrate Freudian parallels to particulars already established in the case of Blake: "Like Blake, Freud . . ."

Blake's writings permit inference of his values for the feminine, but he did not make the critic's work easier by saying, "I use this term in this fashion to mean this, but not this." We do have Freud's specific comments on what he himself regarded as a problem of definition and usage. Like Blake, Freud adopted conventional symbolism and diction for the term "feminine." Unlike Blake, Freud addressed himself directly to the complexities he knew attended that adoption.

Psychoanalysis has a common basis with biology, in that "it presupposes an original bisexuality in human beings. . . . But psychoanalysis cannot elucidate the intrinsic nature of what in conventional or in biological phraseology is termed 'masculine' and 'feminine'; it simply takes over the two concepts and makes them the foundation of its work."[1]

This quotation is taken from the 1920 essay "The Psychogenesis of a Case of Homosexuality in a Woman." But Freud's comments on bisexuality and on the definitions of masculine and feminine are not confined to footnotes in essays from one or another discrete period in his career. He addressed problems of usage and definition as early as 1905 in *Three Essays on the Theory of Sexuality,* and as late as 1937 in "Analysis Terminable and Interminable." Footnotes added to the *Three Essays* over a period of years indicate his continuing concern with a problem he found increasingly troublesome. The hindsight of another decade and another sensibility too readily castigates Freud for what it thinks obvious: that in an area that admittedly provides psychoanalysis with some of the foundation of its work, wholesale adoption of convention is a dangerous inclusion, and the failure to attempt "elucidation" is a suggestive omission. I am a product of that era and that sensibility, but Freud was not; nor was Blake.

Freud was always eager to ally psychoanalysis with biology, but he was also concerned to claim for psychoanalysis an independent status that drew upon but was not limited to biological versions of fact. Freud says he borrowed the idea of bisexuality from reputable scientific sources, but its inclusion in psychoanalytic theory had implications, he well knew, that reached far beyond biology. Since the concept became psychic as well as physiological in the analytic context, it corresponded closely, I think, to current conceptions of androgyny. Androgyny and hermaphroditism are denotatively synonymous, but although the distinction between them has not made its way into standard dictionaries, few people would disagree that there is a connotative difference. Androgyny is primarily a mental and/or spiritual term, while hermaphroditism is fundamentally biological. Freud did not have this nice distinction to draw on, nor did he ever use either term in his discussions of bisexuality. But the psychological attributes he associated with bisexuality are best understood by the contemporary reader in these terms.

The normal evolution of original psychic bisexuality, according to Freud, consists in repression of the characteristics of the opposite sex, which are normally present in all human infants. "It is the attitude belonging to the sex opposite to the subject's own which succumbs to repression."[2] What "attitudes" characterized the feminine and the masculine for Freud? "In maleness is concentrated subject, activity, and the possession of a penis;

femaleness carries on the object, and passivity."[3] But Freud never discussed femininity and masculinity without qualifying himself strenuously in both text and footnotes, precisely because his admittedly arbitrary adoption of conventional terminology was nettlesome to him. In a 1915 footnote added to the 1905 seminal essay "Transformations of Puberty," we find Freud's most comprehensive discussion of the terms:

> It is essential to understand clearly that the concepts of "masculine" and "feminine," whose meaning seems so unambiguous to ordinary people, are among the most confused that occur in science. It is possible to distinguish at least three uses. "Masculine" and "feminine" are sometimes used in the sense of activity and passivity, sometimes in a biological, and sometimes, again, in a sociological sense. The first of these three meanings is the essential one and the most serviceable in psycho-analysis.[4]

The second meaning is purely biological, and is characterized by the presence of spermatozoa or ova, and by the "functions proceeding from them." Activity and its "concomitant phenomena" are linked with "biological masculinity" as a rule; but not always, says Freud, for "there are animal species in which these qualities are on the contrary assigned to the female." The third meaning receives its connotation from "observation of actually existing masculine and feminine individuals."

> Such observation shows that in human beings pure masculinity or pure femininity is not to be found either in a psychological or a biological sense. Every individual . . . displays a mixture of the character traits belonging to his own and to the opposite sex; and he shows a combination of activity and passivity whether or not these last character traits tally with his biological ones.[5]

Bisexuality is among the last things the tolerably well-versed layman will associate with Freud, despite the fact that his comments on it are, as he asserted, "essential" to the understanding of psychoanalysis. Repeatedly Freud stressed that he adopted "masculine" as a synonym for active and "feminine" as a synonym for "passive." Thus identification of "libido," for instance, with masculinity merely meant that libido is active and energetic, not that the presence of libido is normal only in the male. "Both in male and female individuals masculine as well as feminine instinctual impulses are found, and each can equally well undergo repression and so become unconscious."[6] How, then, has Freud been so abysmally misunderstood? Perhaps Freud himself can provide one answer: "For psychology the contrast between the sexes fades away into one between activity and passivity, in which *we far too readily identify activity with maleness and passivity with femaleness,* a view which is by no means universally confirmed in the animal kingdom" (italics mine).[7]

This quotation from *Civilization and Its Discontents* reflects the continuing doubts and also the continuing developments in Freud's later theories regarding masculine and feminine. The younger Freud was content to adopt conventional usage, reminding the reader that he was doing precisely that. A caution, in the form of slight qualification, seemed to him sufficient. In fact, Freud's diction often indicates his sense that he *must* maintain the distinction between femininity and passivity, and *must,* simultaneously, drop the distinction in order to be intelligible in applying his theories to the treatment of real men and real women, who live out and embody both the distinctions and the identifications.

Writing on sadism and masochism in the 1915 *Three Essays,* Freud connects "the simultaneous presence of these opposites with the opposing masculinity and femininity which are combined in bisexuality—a contrast which often has to be replaced in psycho-analysis by that between activity and passivity."[8] He might, indeed, have turned the formulation around, and written that the contrast between activity and passivity must often be replaced by that between masculine and feminine. Freud's theory might retain the pristine categories of activity and passivity, but his practice compelled him to apply those categories to men and women. The sociohistorical and conventional values for femininity and masculinity had, after all, been abstracted from the behavior patterns of men and women. It would take a bolder (and blinder) interpreter of human history than either Blake or Freud to deny that sadism is on intimate terms with activity, masculinity, and males, or that masochism keeps company with passivity, femininity, and women. If one accepts that single example as stated—and I think the burden of proof is on the dissenter—then Freud's qualifications seem somewhat remarkable.

And yet he did make those qualifications, thus indicating that he was always aware of potential dangers in his neat formulations. The older Freud phrases the situation far differently: "We far too readily identify activity with maleness and passivity with femaleness" is an extraordinary statement if one examines its implications for the earlier theoretical edifice, in which Freud declared that analysis "simply takes over the two concepts and makes them the foundation of its work."

Just how much of "the foundation of its work" is based on the identification of masculinity with activity and of femininity with passivity is a matter that might be endlessly disputed. I do not think that the structure of psychoanalysis stands or falls on this point. I do think that the basic model for maturation in men and women as outlined by Freud is profoundly affected by assumptions that deeply disturbed Freud in the final years of his life. I do not, however, think those assumptions adversely affected the accuracy of his theories about "normal" feminine development.

For instance, the "primacy of the phallus" and the labeling of one stage of prepubertal sexual organization as "phallic" is certainly a product of Freud's identification of activity with masculinity. It is important to understand that Freud did not identify activity with masculinity at the pregenital stage. He consistently stated that "an antithesis of trends with active and passive aims" *later* "resolves into the antithesis of male and female."[9]

But resolve into that antithesis it does. Freud's diction is dominated by the blurring of distinctions he might later have wished to retain beyond the pregenital stage of development, and certainly a great many of his unfortunate phrasings are connected to this blurring of distinctions. When he says that "the elimination of clitoridal sexuality is a necessary pre-condition for the development of femininity," he is identifying femininity with receptivity, passivity, and biological reproduction.[10] He was right: normal femininity in his culture was definable by identification with passivity.

All of his formulations regarding the passing of the Oedipus complex in females are dictated by his adoption of conventional terminology. But Freud was anatomizing, analyzing, and dissecting historically determined social and psychic phenomena. A different phrasing might have made contemporary feminist critics happier, but it would not have changed the facts. When Freud says that normal female development is split into two phases, the first "masculine," the second "specifically feminine," he is saying no more and no less than that the first stage is active, the second passive.[11]

Furthermore, Freud's choice of terminology also served, ironically, to preserve certain distinctions that are of considerable value to the contemporary reader. He calls the "lack" of the penis the "negative character of [the female] sex," and he has been condemned for such seemingly judgment-loaded lingo. But that phraseology reflects the value judgments of both men and women toward "femininity." Regarding that projection from the male body and the problems it seems to have caused between men and women, Alfred Alder suggested that the term "masculine protest" be adopted to signify both the wish for the penis in women and the struggle against passivity in men. Freud preferred to retain the phrase "repudiation of femininity."[12] Either term might arguably serve the purpose, and Adler's includes connotations less unpleasant to some readers. Freud's is more brutal, but it is also more accurate in its depiction of attitudes toward femininity traditionally shared by men and women.

Would it have made no difference at all, then, if Freud had sooner recognized the implications of his language? On the contrary, I think the danger that troubled him was real, but it oper-

ates on a deeper level than that of language. Freud's choice of
words was the linguistic representation of his own and his culture's processes of symbol formation. Freud's own contributions
to our knowledge of psychic processes permit us to perceive that
the problem was deeper than language, that in fact it has its
sources in the evolution of consciousness as a gender-specific
phenomenon. As a fully enculturated male member of a patriarchal society, Freud was not able to analyze as "objectively" as
an outsider might. He could see that the identification of
females with characteristics regarded as feminine was problematic, but he could not escape the fact that he had accepted that
identification as part of the structure of his consciousness. And
the basic structure was well established before he possessed the
requisite mental development to examine the structure of consciousness and its relationship to unconscious, unacknowledged
mental processes.

His theory maintained the distinction between active/passive
trends and masculine/feminine in the pregenital stage; but their
"resolution" into masculine and feminine characteristics as dis-
played by males and females indicates that such resolution was
literally foretold and prefigured; that, in other words, the carefully maintained distinction was only arbitrary, and only theoretical. Like Blake, he could see that humans had always identified
certain characteristics as masculine, certain others as feminine,
and like Blake, he possessed the insight to demonstrate to others
how that identification operated in their lives. And finally, also
like Blake, he could not foresee how deeply he was caught in the
same determined and deterministic trap. When Freud writes
that women "lack" a penis, and that this lack is the "negative"
character of the female sex, he employs language I find useful
and accurate as a reflection of attitudes toward and definitions
of femininity. The only thing "wrong" with such diction is that
he believed it himself.

We can see this complex situation operating in many of
Freud's case-history discussions. In "The Psychogenesis of a
Case of Homosexuality in a Woman," Freud writes: "Some of

her intellectual attributes also could be connected with masculinity: for instance, her acuteness of comprehension and her lucid objectivity, in so far as she was not dominated by her passion; though these distinctions are conventional rather than scientific."[13] He makes the immediate connection of intelligence and "objectivity" with masculinity, and implicitly comments on her "feminine" characteristics as well by qualifying that objectivity. "Passion," apparently, is "feminine." Any reader will know what Freud means here, for these assumptions are so deeply and continuously shared that no historical gloss on the term is necessary. He means that her objectivity is sometimes clouded by irrational feelings. Even if this discussion had not been preceded by an explication of Freud's system, we would also know that Freud (and men, and women, and culture) value "objectivity" more highly than "passion." Passion is the pejorative version of affectivity and emotiveness, which even in their positive manifestations are less valued by a patriarchal society than their "masculine" antitheses.

The passage also includes one somewhat paradoxical problem in terminology. Freud, who always flirted with the idea of calling "libido" a masculine category because it was active and energetic by definition, never seemed to question his own and his culture's connection of irrationally manifested libido with femininity, that is, passion. Like the good scientist he is, Freud perceives that he has used language sloppily, so he makes a qualification that amounts to partial retraction: "these distinctions are conventional rather than scientific." He does not go on to suggest ways of speaking about this woman that will clarify her case in a purely scientific way; rather, he proceeds to use language that, while less sloppy and less obviously connotative, is also less honest. In other words, when he is being what he fancies purely "scientific," as opposed to conventional, he makes the same comments and uses the same value judgments, but without admitting he is doing so. Freud knew very well that the language of science *is* conventional—"the concepts of masculine and feminine are among the most confused that occur in science"— but he wished it were not so.

Finally, the careful qualification Freud employs in this passage rings false. We know that the patient's "intellectual attributes" not only "could be" connected with masculinity; in Freud's own thinking, they are. It is no wonder that he did not go on to question the fundamentals of his own theories, given his troubled perception that there might be something amiss in his thinking. Perhaps the wonder is that it ever occurred to him to think there might be something amiss.

Freud's comments on the phenomenon of sexual overvaluation in "The Sexual Aberrations" (*Three Essays on the Theory of Sexuality*) provide another example of his confusion, though this time without any apparent awareness on his part that his use of terminology is problematic. He finds that sexual overvaluation is best studied in men, because that characteristic in women is "still veiled in an impenetrable obscurity . . . partly owing to the stunting effect of civilized conditioning, and partly owing to their conventional secretiveness and insincerity."[14] Freud's frequent comments on "civilized conditioning" indicate a sympathetic awareness of its effects on women. In this respect, he was positively egalitarian; I can find no indication that he thought men more crushed or stunted than women, or more deserving of sympathy.

What this statement lacks is an awareness of connections between the conjunctive clauses. His mention of "conventional secretiveness and insincerity" is not necessarily judgmental, but his lack of comment connecting those characteristics to "the stunting effect of civilized conditioning" is, I think, at least implicitly judgmental. There is another value judgment implicit in this passage, a far subtler one than might be inferred from his characterization of women as conventionally secretive and insincere. Freud was interested in the tendency of men to overvalue the love object, and he developed a terminology designed to express various kinds and degrees of relationship with and dependence on the love object. In his essay "On Narcissism," Freud discussed "complete object love" marked by "sexual overestimation," and ventured to suggest that it is normally characteristic only of the male.[15] He called this kind of love "anaclitic," and discoursed on its effects in a number of essays. His amusement at the prospect of intelligent, cultured men declaring their unworthiness of superficial, dumb-bunny women was probably justified in many cases. But his readily aroused incredulity is so consistent that it is difficult to avoid the conclusion that Freud thought women seldom worthy of men. Perhaps his clientele justified that assumption on his part; and if so, his assumption of innate feminine inferiority probably prevented him from further investigating those "stunting effects of civilized conditioning" on women.

Since Freud did doubt his own categories of usage for feminine and masculine, and more so as the years passed, why did he not take his questioning a step or two or three further? One obvious answer is that he was growing old and becoming ill by the time he came seriously to question himself. He just didn't have enough time. In this area more than in any other, Freud willingly admitted his insecurity. He also willingly and justifiably excused himself. In "The Passing of the Oedipus Complex" (1924) he writes, "It must be confessed, however, that on the whole our insight into these processes of development in the girl is unsatisfying, shadowy, and incomplete."[16] Posterity will have to handle this one, says Freud.

It was a favorite rhetorical strategy of Freud's to step aside modestly when he really intended no such thing. But on this subject he was sincere, because he was genuinely bothered by the insufficiency of his own findings. In "Female Sexuality," his 1931 summary essay on the findings of analysis regarding feminine psychology, he thought it proper to "admit that we have not yet got to the bottom of processes which, after all, we have only come to know of."[17] Ironically, he does not repeat in this essay his uneasiness with the analytic usage of the terms "masculine" and "feminine." It is as if he saw the two issues as related but distinctly separate.

The most significant source of Freud's failure to take his self-questioning further is the same source that prevented him from envisioning art as a way out of the closed system. I refer to the naturalistic determinism examined at length in this study, and to his desire to make of psychoanalysis a natural science rather than a dynamically creative art. Psychoanalysis *is* a dynamically creative art, but one that is always rooted by its founder to the rock-solid natural-science foundation he thought necessary for its survival in the coming age. Psychoanalysis was to be the science of the mind that would correspond in general validity and in particulars to the science of the body. He knew that science was not truly "objective," and it was often on the very subject of definitions for masculine and feminine and their relationship to male and female that he pointed out the subjectivity of scientific language. He even turned to biology for his evidence that sexual dialectics were indeed more complex than either loosely social or tightly scientific usages acknowledged, as we have also seen. But to follow out the ultimate implications of such insights would have been to dethrone the objectivity of "science," and that illusion of objectivity was too dear for Freud to give up.

The results of Freud's passionate romance with biology were comprehensive. I have discussed the results of that romance in terms of Freud's reluctance to be a visionary and a prophet. The ultimate enslavement of man to nature is also, for Freud, the ultimate enslavement of woman. In "The Passing of the Oedipus Complex," Freud wrote: "The feministic demand for equal rights between the sexes does not carry far here; the morphological difference must express itself in differences in the development of the mind. 'Anatomy is Destiny,' to vary a saying of Napoleon's."[18] Freud's currency with female readers has suffered incalculably as a result of that statement. His assertion has provided them an occasion to ignore the validity of many of his theories on feminine psychology.

But in fact, I believe it is still a minority of women, and men, who do not think that the "development of the mind" is gender-related. Even the nature–nurture dispute seems always destined to dissolve into tautologies. Perhaps a more advanced biology will provide absolute answers to the relationship between nature and nurture in the sexes. I do not wish to quarrel with, or even to fault, Freud's statement that morphological differences "express themselves" in mental differences. Anatomy is, in some nearly indisputable respects, destiny, and for everyone, male and female alike. (We all die somatically, at the very least.) If there is anything regrettable in Freud's passage from my point of view, it is the use of biology implicitly to define those analogous differences in body and mind in the sexes, and in a way that needlessly limits biological as well as psychological fact. Freud's attempt to make psychic reality correspond on a one-to-one basis with biological reality suggests that since the female in nature is passive-receptive, the female in culture will be "naturally" the same. Was it not to biology that Freud turned for his examples to show that, for instance, passivity and femininity are not necessarily the same? Freud not only constrained his theory of the mind to a natural model; he also constrained the natural model.

Another difficulty in Freud's thinking presents itself with the use of the somatic-mental parallel as a conclusive proof that "equal rights" are untenable. This statement suggests that social institutions must follow natural ones, and that natural differences are inevitably hierarchical. Things-as-they-are becomes its own justification. This is the same mind that so painstakingly enumerated the noble qualities that differentiate civilization from the barbarous natural state, the same mind that so highly valued what he called "ideas," the same mind that castigated civilization for the retrogressive bias that continually betrayed its own "highest" aims.

Freud knew that nature had not an "idea" in her head, that symbol formation belonged to mankind alone. He knew, in other words, that nature was "feminine" only because mankind personified it as woman, as idea. He created psychoanalysis because natural science did not account for ideas, symbols, metaphors, and because nature was an inadequate model for mind. But finally, Freud could not outgrow his acolytic attitude toward nature and her science, which promised that illusory objectivity his own discipline anatomized. He worshiped her as a goddess, and her students were the priests among whom he counted himself. In short, Freud could not help being a man. "Wherever primitive man institutes a taboo, there he fears a danger; and it cannot be disputed that the general principle underlying all these regulations and avoidances is a dread of woman.... There is nothing in all this which is extinct, which is not still alive in the heart of man today."[19]

I interpret Freud's reluctance to question further his own categories and definitions of masculine and feminine and his failure to apply his own methodology to his theories on feminine psychology as a self-imposed taboo. That taboo was "inherited," to use Freud's own quasi-biological terminology, through centuries of male conditioning and conventional enculturation. Freud was in the business of breaking taboos; that is how he earned his livelihood and his reputation as a man of great mind. He overcame barriers that look, at first glance, higher than this one, for he confronted the idea of incest, of murder, of self-destructiveness in himself as well as in human history. But this taboo was even more comprehensive, for it had to do with anomaly, with the crossing of boundaries that, once truly traversed, might leave man and woman with no definable identities at all.

Freud worried at the corners of the problem all of his life. His belief in "original bisexuality" was a huge step in the direction of confronting the meaning of masculine and feminine, and his troubled qualification of terminology was another. But activity and passivity do resolve into masculine and feminine for Freud, and for all his later assertions that men may adopt passive attitudes and women active ones, Freud always describes such attitudes as "feminine attributes" in a fundamentally masculine being, and vice versa. I think this proclivity was partially rooted in his need irrefutably to identify himself as man, and his need to have some definitive idea of what being a man means.

"Wherever ... man institutes a taboo, there he fears a danger," and that danger is always, according to Freud, a dread of woman. If Freud were to have questioned further the meanings of masculine and feminine, the danger to himself, and to all men, would have been virtually incalculable. Power, privilege,

authority, objectivity, exclusivity—all might have had to be forfeited. Or at least the "right" to it all would have had to be
forfeited, and Freud was an upright and good man. If he had
come to closer terms with the issue, it might have destroyed him.
It might also, in his own eyes if not in mine, have destroyed his
confidence in his work, which comes to destruction of the man.
"There is nothing in all this which is . . . not still alive in the heart
of man today." Open admission of other fears and insecurities
are plentiful in Freud, but this one remained largely unconscious and pervasive.

"Analysis Terminable and Interminable," published in 1937,
two years before his death, was one of Freud's last major essays.
In it he discussed the most pressing problems of psychoanalysis
as he saw them, and those problems are, of course, related to the
efficacy of psychoanalytic treatment. It is not surprising to find
that this essay is thoroughly infused with biological phrasings
and with aggressively self-limiting statements about the province
of psychoanalysis. Freud considers the theories of Empedocles,
and concludes that they were so close to his own that he would be
tempted to say that the two were identical were it not for the fact
that "the Greek's theory is a cosmic phantasy, while our own
confines its application to biology." He further states, in a dependent clause, that psychoanalysis is "necessarily restricted to
the biopsychical field."[20] Freud's circle has grown smaller and
tighter over the years. My major interest in this essay is its recapitulation of an ultimate problem in psychoanalytic theory and
practice.

In the final section of the essay, Freud writes about "the prominence of two themes which give the analyst an extraordinary
amount of trouble." These two themes, "connected with the difference between the sexes," are penis envy in women and the
struggle against passivity or the "feminine attitude" in men. The
common element in these two troublesome themes is the "repudiation of femininity."[21] One desirable outcome of the
psychoanalytic process is the resolution of this problem, that is,
the abandonment of the wish for a penis in women and the

acceptance of occasional passivity as a useful attitude in men. In other words, Freud is discussing the attempt of psychoanalysis to allay the pejorative connotations of femininity for both men and women. No one, apparently, wants to be "feminine" if feminine means passive, for passivity always operates in opposition to activity, and therefore becomes a power issue: if you are passive, you are object, not subject.

Freud employs a deliberate understatement (primarily as a courtesy to Ferenczi, who thought that such resolution was absolutely definitional to psychoanalytic cure) when he says of this ideal: "I think Ferenczi was asking a very great deal." Freud thought this resolution very unlikely to occur, and it caused him the deepest misgivings about the efficacy of psychoanalysis. He wrote that this issue was the "bedrock" of cure, for "in the psychical field the biological factor is really the rock-bottom. The repudiation of femininity must surely be a biological fact, part of the great riddle of sex." Freud knew, then, that psychoanalysis most often failed itself and its patients right here. But the moment the magic word "biology" occurs, Freud cannot think what else to do. It is indeed "rock-bottom": there is no way out and no way up. His female patients feel an "inner conviction that the analysis will avail them nothing and that they will be none the better for it." And he agrees with them, when their "strongest motive" for treatment was the "hope that they might still obtain a male organ, the lack of which is so painful to them." What is to be done, then? "Analysis Terminable and Interminable" ends with the sadly resigned comment that analysts must "console themselves" that "everything possible has been done to encourage the patient to examine and to change his attitude to the question."[22]

The contemporary reader, of course, will want to substitute the word "analyst" for "patient" in the last clause. We will rush to Ruth Moulton and Karen Horney, and suggest that Freud should have been less literal in his interpretation of penis envy. Rephrased as "power envy, the concept will be accepted even by the feminists as an inevitable factor in the psychic life of women.

It seems so little to ask, just a tiny bit of metaphor sprinkled into the biological soup. But Freud clung tenaciously to the literal letter and the protruding gland. Was he wrong? I think not. The term "power envy" sounds more comprehensive than penis envy, but in fact, penis envy (or Freud's most commonly used phrase for it, "the wish for a penis") always included power envy for Freud. The body-specific term is the more inclusive of the two concepts.

If Freud had capitulated to pressures to generalize his terminology, in this specific example and in many others, psychoanalysis would have told its public little that was new or even interesting. Women envy the power of men? Yes, but that was hardly news in early-twentieth-century Western Europe. The repressed wish for a penis often controls the psychic lives of women? That's news. But in addition to being more newsworthy, Freud's formulation had the considerable advantage of illuminating the relationship between maturity and infancy and between consciousness and unconsciousness. The most significant reason for keeping the terminology untouched, then, is that it thus more accurately accounts for psychic processes. The same can be said for the specificity of "repudiation of femininity." It is not merely that men do not want to be passive; it is that men do not want to be women, for that is what passivity means to them.

My loyalty to Freud's biological terminology might seem to contradict my obviously negative attitude toward Freud's enslavement to biology. I am sympathetic to those who wish to change penis envy to power envy. It would have been nicer if Freud had changed it, and with it, perhaps, some of his attitudes toward femininity. But then Freud would not have been Freud, and psychoanalysis would be even fuzzier than it is. The real problem, as I see it, is somewhat different.

I turn again to the difference between prophet and analyst which began my reading of Blake and Freud. The analyst must see things as they are and as they have been. Freud did exactly that, and his alliance with biology probably did as much to assist that analysis as to restrict it. But the prophet, looking at his own analysis, refuses to regard the natural as bedrock. Has no one thought of a way out? Then, says the prophet, we must think of a new idea, another metaphor, a fresh imagining. Blake's predicament regarding values for the feminine was much like Freud's. He adopted conventional terminology in order to analyze, and that terminology and the symbol formations it represented were enough like Freud's that both men's pessimistic view of cultural transformation is amply justified. There is a century between them, but both men had to say the same things to equally unsympathetic publics, and in the very different worlds of science and poetry.

Both men knew that this "great riddle of sex" was The Problem that included all other problems. Both men knew that the sexes had done a fine job of making each other and themselves quite miserable, even if they had managed to do little else. And both men knew that if there was any telling transformation possible in culture, it must be a sexual transformation. Like doctors diagnosing and treating a terrible plague, they ran the risk of catching their death of it. Or, rather, they were born with the disease as surely as the people they tried to treat, though both of them seemed not quite aware of this.

Blake became aware of it in his later career, and the diagnostician turned visionary. He could not rid himself of the profoundly negative associations with femininity that resulted from its cultural identification with nature, passivity, and mindlessness. So, instead, he began to envision new possibilities and values for femininity by changing his point of view. Each negative value might have its imaginatively positive analogue. Women and feminine principles became the ability to move between time and space, and between humanity and humanity. His bitter lack of reverence for nature made it easier for him to be less deterministic in imagining new values for femininity, even if it also bound him to revile the aspect of femininity that had always been associated with the natural.

This is, of course, what I wish Freud could have done. I see why he could not. The reasons are the same ones that kept him from embracing art as an escape from determinism. I do not wish that he had changed his analysis of patriarchy, for I consider it incalculably valuable and demonstrably correct. Freud, old and dying in 1937, was sadly distressed about the future of his science. If he had perceived himself as creative artist as well as scientist, his entire notion of cure would certainly have been profoundly different. Freud thought his idea of cure realistic and theoretically attainable, for it consisted of advantageous compromises among constituents of the personality, and between the ego and the outside world. "The business of analysis," he wrote, "is to secure the best possible psychological conditions for the functioning of the ego; when this has been done, analysis has accomplished its task."[23] That best possible functioning ideally included unrestricted capacity for enjoyment and productivity, but this was seldom the case. "Best possible," he seemed to say in "Analysis Terminable and Interminable," was more often damned poor. Far from thinking his ideal too restricted, Freud thought it ultimately too expansive.

It may be unkind to wish that such a rebel as Freud had been more rebellious. The final rebellion, of course, would have been to turn away from nature when he reached the boundaries of its usefulness for psychology, and to attempt a radical reevaluation of masculine and feminine. If so many women protested that being "feminine" did not feel "natural" to them, perhaps Freud's unique resources and historical situation could have begun the long, slow process of changing not only the values of what has been traditionally regarded as feminine but also the content of those values. But a wish is one thing, a justified expectation quite another.

Afterword: New Jerusalem and Old Rome

What do I see? The Briton Saxon Roman Norman amalgamating
In my Furnaces into One Nation the English: & taking Refuge
In the Loins of Albion. The Canaanite united with the fugitive
Hebrew, whom She divided into Twelve. & sold into Egypt
Then scatterd the Egyptian & Hebrew to the four Winds:
This sinful Nation Created in our Furnaces & Looms is Albion
So Los spoke. Enitharmon answerd in great terror in Lambeths Vale

The Poets Song draws to its period & Enitharmon is no more.
For if he be that Albion I can never weave him in my Looms
But when he touches the first fibrous thread. like filmy dew

Jerusalem

Thy Looms will be no more & I annihilate vanish for ever
Then thou wilt Create another Female according to thy Will.

Los answerd swift as the shuttle of gold. Sexes must vanish & cease
To be, when Albion arises from his dread repose O lovely Enitharmon:
When all their Crimes, their Punishments their Accusations of Sin:
All their Jealousies Revenges Murders. hidings of Cruelty in Deceit
Appear only in the Outward Spheres of Visionary Space and Time.
In the shadows of Possibility by Mutual Forgiveness forevermore
And in the Vision & in the Prophecy that we may Foresee & Avoid
The terrors of Creation & Redemption & Judgment. Beholding them
Displayd in the Emanative Visions of Canaan in Jerusalem & in Shiloh
And in the Shadows of Remembrance. & in the Chaos of the Spectre
Amalek, Edom, Egypt, Moab, Ammon, Ashur, Philistea, around Jerusalem
Where the Druids reard their Rocky Circles to make permanent Remembrance
Of Sin. & the Tree of Good & Evil sprang from the Rocky Circle & Snake
Of the Druid, along the Valley of Rephaim from Camberwell to Golgotha
And framed the Mundane Shell Cavernous in Length Bredth & Highth

The Resurrection of Jerusalem. From William Blake, *Jerusalem*, Plate 92
(1804–18). Relief etching. Library of Congress, Rosenwald Collection.

The imaginations of both Blake and Freud were moved by the idea of cities. For Blake, the sunlit city was Eternity. The pastoral vision did not touch him. "Where man is not, nature is barren." Freud, even if he was bound to nature by self-made manacles, also rejected the pastoral ideal. Both were urban men who lived their adult lives primarily in a single city. For Freud, the city was Vienna; for Blake, London. But each man was compelled by the vision of a city of the imagination. Blake's was the New Jerusalem, the city of apocalyptic redemption in a spiritual future, and Freud's was Old Rome, the city of artistic and imperial glory in a material past. Blake never visited the material Jerusalem, but that did not matter. His Jerusalem was the city of Revelation and of his own mythopoeic vision, "a city yet a woman." Jerusalem is the emanation of everything human for Blake, the mediatrix between humanity and regenerated nature, the ever present potential for movement and growth. She is the artist's vision, the poet's words, and the lover's love, the completely humanized form of everything.

Freud did visit his city of the imagination, but it was not the living Rome that compelled him. It was for ruined Rome that he expressed a continued fascination and affection. His collection of Roman reproductions was undoubtedly his most prized material possession. Rome's ancient ruins held for him the same kind of fascination that mankind's ancient psychic ruins held. His theory demonstrated that those psychic ruins were actually alive and well and living in us all. Once he tried to bring to life the city's ruins as well. In *Civilization and Its Discontents,* Freud attempts to explain mental life in analogy with the Eternal City.

He is trying to express his belief that "in mental life, nothing which has once been formed can perish."

> Now let us, by a flight of imagination, suppose that Rome is not a human habitation but a psychical entity with a similarly long and copious past—an entity, that is to say, in which nothing which has once come into existence will have passed away and all the earlier phases of development continue to exist alongside the latest ones.[1]

The ensuing paragraph imagines what such a city might look like. It would be alive, just as is a human being, with past and present. "Where the Coliseum now stands we could at the same time admire Nero's vanished Golden House." Freud indulges this fancy for many sentences, telling us that "the observer would perhaps only have to change the direction of his glance or his position in order to call up the one view or the other."[2] Suddenly, almost rudely, Freud calls a halt to this phantasy, on the grounds that chronology cannot be understood in spatial terms, for "the same space cannot have two different contents."

> There is clearly no point in spinning our phantasy any further, for it leads to things that are unimaginable and even absurd.... Our attempt seems to be an idle game. It has only one justification. It shows us how far we are from mastering the characteristics of mental life by representing them in pictorial terms.... A city is thus *a priori* unsuited for a comparison of this sort with a mental organism.[3]

The practiced reader of Freud begins looking for him to pick up the game again. That diction—"seems to be an idle game"—is usually a fair indicator that Freud is playing another kind of game with the reader, one in which he will skillfully bring the reader to the conclusion that nothing *but* a city is suited for comparison with a mental organism. But that expectation will be frustrated. Gametime is really over, and it's curtains for the dead city that Freud brought to brief life in his "flight of imagination." Freud would probably be surprised to know that this dropped analogy is among the best known of his flights of imagination.

He dropped it for good reason, of course. It was dangerous, he felt, to restrict sequential phenomena to spatial confines. But his justification does not concern me here. I am interested in that metaphoric, artistic, creative, poetic, imaginative turn of mind that Freud never entirely trusted in himself, the same turn of mind that Blake put all his trust in. Blake *did* master the characteristics of mental life "by representing them in pictorial terms." For Blake, the same space *could* have two different contents. For Blake, the city remained alive, and hosted the resurrection of human hope. For Freud, the living city died, falling into fascinating ruins—but ruins nevertheless. "He became what he beheld." What Freud beheld at the end of his life was not the glory of an imaginative Rome but the desiccation of the real Vienna. Murray Schwartz wrote on an earlier draft of this study: "Think what the world must have looked like to a Jew dying of throat cancer in Nazi-occupied Vienna." I think of that, and then I understand Freud's pessimism, and love him for the modicum of hope and vision he retained. Life was hard on Blake, but harder, finally, on Freud.

I think of one final thing. Freud and Blake both died in London, which was another Jerusalem for Blake. London was the city of literal deliverance for Freud, but it never meant to him what Rome had always meant. When I think of Freud's Rome, it is the Rome of this short passage in *Civilization and Its Discontents,* and it represents, for me, all the possibilities still inherent in psychoanalysis. Those possibilities are the same ones Blake offered, and they are always present in art and love. I disregard Freud's warning, and indeed, it leads to things "unimaginable and even absurd." Rome becomes Jerusalem.

Notes

Introduction

1. Richard King, *The Party of Eros: Radical Social Thought and the Realm of Freedom* (Chapel Hill: University of North Carolina Press, 1972).

2. King, *Party of Eros,* p. 44.

3. King, *Party of Eros,* p. 47.

4. Wilhelm Reich, *The Sexual Revolution* (New York: Farrar, Straus & Giroux, Noonday Press, 1962).

5. Reich, *Sexual Revolution,* p. 14.

6. Juliet Mitchell, *Psychoanalysis and Feminism: Freud, Reich, Laing, and Women* (New York: Pantheon Books, 1974). See pt. 2, sec. 1, pp. 137–226.

7. Reich, *Character Analysis* (New York: Noonday Press, 1967), p. 15.

8. Reich, *Character Analysis,* Preface to 2d ed. (1945), p. xviii.

9. Herbert Marcuse, *Eros and Civilization: A Philosophical Inquiry into Freud* (Boston: Beacon Press, 1955, 1966), p. 3.

10. Marcuse, *Eros and Civilization,* pp. 4–5.

11. For a detailed discussion of the relationship between "performance principle" and "reality principle," see Marcuse, *Eros and Civilization,* chaps. 2, 4, and 6.

12. Marcuse, *Eros and Civilization,* p. 5.

13. Marcuse, *Eros and Civilization,* pp. 142–43.

14. Marcuse, *Eros and Civilization,* p. 159.

15. Marcuse, *Eros and Civilization,* pp. 179, 199.

16. Marcuse, *Eros and Civilization,* p. 201.

17. See especially my discussion of Blake's *Visions of the Daughters of Albion,* Chapter 4.

18. Marcuse, *Eros and Civilization,* p. 11.

19. Marcuse, *Eros and Civilization,* p. 164.

20. Marcuse, *Eros and Civilization*, pp. 162–70.

21. Norman O. Brown, *Life against Death* (New York: Vintage Books, 1959), p. 242.

22. Brown, *Love's Body* (New York: Vintage Books, 1966), p. 23.

23. Brown, *Love's Body*, p. 145.

24. Brown, *Love's Body*, pp. 233, 239.

25. King, *Party of Eros*, p. 7.

26. King, *Party of Eros*, p. 7.

27. June Singer's reading in *The Unholy Bible: A Psychological Interpretation of William Blake* (New York: Colophon Books, 1970) works for *The Marriage of Heaven and Hell*, but not so well for the later prophecies. For further comments on Singer, see p. 246. Christine Gallant's *Blake and the Assimilation of Chaos* (Princeton: Princeton University Press, 1978) came to my attention while this book was in press. Gallant usefully employs Jungian archetypes to explicate Blake.

28. See Naomi Weisstein, Virginia Blaisdell, and Jesse Lemisch, *The Godfathers: Freudians, Marxists, and the Scientific and Political Protection Societies* (New Haven, Conn.: Belladonna Publishing, 1975). The discussion of Freud on pp. 61–85 is illuminating as a summary of the mainline feminist position on Freud: "To exhume Freud, whose theories have been proven useless, . . . seems to us to reflect an astonishing and dangerous ignorance, and a deep anti-scientific and anti-intellectual bias. . . . It's not just that he's vicious towards women; more important, he's *wrong*, not just about women, but about humans in general" (pp. 74, 75).

29. Leo Bersani, *Baudelaire and Freud* (Berkeley: University of California Press, 1977), p. 4n.

30. Bersani, *Baudelaire and Freud*, p. 5.

1. Opposition Is True Friendship

1. Sigmund Freud, *Civilization and Its Discontents*, trans. and ed. James Strachey (New York: Norton, 1962), pp. 91–92. Strachey bases his translation on the first English translation of the work by Joan Riviere (London: Hogarth Press and Institute of Psychoanalysis, 1930). As my discussion of Freud in this and subsequent chapters refers to a number of essays, books, editions, and translations, inclusion of pertinent information in the text of the discussion would be intrusive rather than helpful to the reader. I have therefore adopted a uniform policy of confining citations to the notes, even when several consecutive citations are taken from the same essay, edition, and translation.

2. Freud, "'Civilized' Sexual Morality and Modern Nervousness" (1908), trans. E. B. Herford and E. Colburn Mayne, in *Collected Papers of Sigmund Freud*, ed. Ernest Jones, 5 vols. (New York: Basic Books, 1959), II, 99.

3. Freud, "A Special Type of Object Choice Made by Men" (1910), trans. Joan Riviere, from "Contributions to the Psychology of Love," in *Collected Papers*, IV, 193.

4. Freud, *Civilization and Its Discontents*, p. 30.

5. Freud, *Civilization and Its Discontents*, p. 33.

6. Freud, *Civilization and Its Discontents*, p. 40.

7. Freud, *Civilization and Its Discontents*, p. 30.

8. Freud, *Civilization and Its Discontents*, p. 30.

9. Freud, *Civilization and Its Discontents*, p. 67. "Denn die Kindlein, Sie hören es nicht gerne." According to Strachey, Freud takes the quotation from Goethe's poem "Die Ballade vom vertriebenen und heimgekehrten Grafen."

10. Freud, "Female Sexuality" (1931), trans. Joan Riviere, in *Collected Papers*, V, 262.

11. Freud, *An Autobiographical Study*, trans. James Strachey (New York: Norton, 1963), p. 122.

12. Freud, *Civilization and Its Discontents*, p. 27.

13. See, for instance, "The Theme of the Three Caskets" (1913), in *Collected Papers*, IV, 244–56; "The Moses of Michelangelo" (1914), in *Collected Papers*, IV, 257–87; and "Dostoevsky and Parricide" (1928), in *Collected Papers*, V, 222–42.

14. Freud, "Formulations Regarding the Two Principles in Mental Functioning (1911)," trans. M. N. Searl, in *Collected Papers*, IV, 19.

15. Freud, "The Moses of Michelangelo" (1914), trans. Alix Strachey, in *Collected Papers*, IV, 257.

16. Freud, "The Relation of the Poet to Day-Dreaming" (1908), trans. I. F. Grant Duff, in *Collected Papers*, IV, 178.

17. Freud, "The Unconscious" (1915), trans. Cecil Baines, in *Collected Papers*, IV, 119.

18. Freud, *Totem and Taboo*, trans. A. A. Brill (New York: Random House, 1946), p. 83.

19. Freud, *Totem and Taboo*, p. 85.

20. Freud, *Totem and Taboo*, p. 103.

21. Freud, *Totem and Taboo*, p. 101.

22. Freud, *Totem and Taboo*, pp. 99, 101.

23. Freud, *Totem and Taboo*, pp. 115, 118.

24. Freud, *Totem and Taboo*, p. 119.

25. Freud, *Totem and Taboo*, p. 118.

26. Freud, *Civilization and Its Discontents,* p. 92.

27. Freud, *Totem and Taboo,* p. 44.

28. Freud, " 'Civilized' Sexual Morality," p. 92.

29. Freud, *Civilization and Its Discontents,* p. 81n, and "Types of Neurotic Nosogenesis" (1912), trans. E. Colburn Mayne, in *Collected Papers,* II, 118.

30. Joyce Cary, *The Horse's Mouth* (New York: Harper & Row, 1965), p. 345. *The Horse's Mouth,* first published in 1944, is the concluding novel in Cary's *First Trilogy,* of which the first and second novels are *Herself Surprised* and *To Be a Pilgrim.* Gulley Jimson is Cary's version of Blake's Los, the iconoclastic prophet and visionary who "keeps the divine vision in time of trouble."

2. They Became What They Beheld

1. William Blake, "A Vision of the Last Judgment."

2. Blake, "There Is No Natural Religion (*b*)."

3. Blake, *Europe.*

4. Sigmund Freud, *The Ego and the Id,* in *A General Selection from the Works of Sigmund Freud,* ed. John Rickman, trans. Joan Riviere (Garden City, N.Y.: Doubleday Anchor Books, 1957), p. 227.

5. Sigmund Freud, *Civilization and Its Discontents,* trans. and ed. James Strachey (New York: Norton, 1962), p. 23.

6. Freud, "Analysis Terminable and Interminable" (1937), trans. Joan Riviere, in *Collected Papers of Sigmund Freud,* ed. Ernest Jones, 5 vols. (New York: Basic Books, 1959), V, 316.

7. Freud, *The Ego and the Id,* p. 222.

8. I expect that my patently reductionist formulation here is sufficiently qualified by the discussion that follows.

9. Freud, "The Unconscious" (1915), in *Collected Papers,* IV, 99.

10. Freud, *Beyond the Pleasure Principle,* ed. Gregory Zilboorg, trans. James Strachey (New York: Bantam Books, 1972), pp. 70, 68.

11. Freud, "Analysis Terminable and Interminable" (1937), pp. 342, 345.

12. Constricted perception, under the tyranny of the natural eye, determines being-in-nature as a fallen state. Of the many studies that explore in depth Blake's views on perception and cognition, the best is Thomas Frosch, *The Awakening of Albion* (Ithaca: Cornell University Press, 1974). Frosch's insights also inform my approach to feminine metaphors in Blake.

3. Innocence and Experience

1. Sigmund Freud, *The Problem of Anxiety*, trans. Henry Alden Bunker (New York: Psychoanalytic Quarterly Press and W. W. Norton, 1963), pp. 108-9.

2. Freud, "Female Sexuality," trans. Joan Riviere, in *Collected Papers of Sigmund Freud*, ed. Ernest Jones, 5 vols. (New York: Basic Books, 1959), V, 258, 259.

3. Freud, "Types of Neurotic Nosogenesis" (1912), trans. E. Colburn Mayne, in *Collected Papers*, II, 118.

4. Freud, "On Narcissism," trans. Cecil M. Baines, in *Collected Papers*, IV, 51.

5. Freud, "On Narcissism," pp. 35-36.

6. Freud, "On Narcissism," p. 57.

7. Freud, "On Narcissism," p. 52.

8. For Freud's discussions of this point, see especially *Problem of Anxiety*.

9. Bataille's *Death and Sensuality* is a study of eroticism, taboo, mysticism, and literature. Bataille's credibility suffers from incoherent translations, but his somewhat wiggy theses are valuable to the psychoanalytic critic.

10. Freud, *The Ego and the Id*, in *A General Selection from the Works of Sigmund Freud*, ed. John Rickman, trans. Joan Riviere (Garden City, N.Y.: Doubleday Anchor Books, 1957), p. 215.

11. Freud, "On Narcissism," pp. 46-47.

12. Freud, "The Passing of the Oedipus Complex" (1924), trans. Joan Riviere, in *Collected Papers*, II, 271.

13. Freud, "On Narcissism," p. 49.

14. Freud, "Female Sexuality," p. 257.

15. Freud, *Ego and the Id*, p. 222.

16. Freud, *Civilization and Its Discontents*, trans. and ed. James Strachey (New York: Norton, 1962), p. 42.

17. Freud, "'Civilized' Sexual Morality and Modern Nervousness" (1908), trans. E. B. Herford and E. Colburn Mayne, in *Collected Papers*, II, 83-85.

18. Freud, "'Civilized' Sexual Morality," pp. 76, 80.

19. Freud, "'Civilized' Sexual Morality," pp. 76-77.

20. Freud, "'Civilized' Sexual Morality," p. 82.

21. Freud, "Passing of the Oedipus Complex," p. 273.

22. Freud, *Civilization and Its Discontents*, p. 31.

23. Freud, "My Views on the Part Played by Sexuality in the Aetiology of the Neuroses" (1905), trans J. Bernays, in *Collected Papers*, I, 281.

24. Freud, *Ego and the Id,* p. 228.

25. Freud, *Ego and the Id,* p. 222.

26. Freud, *Civilization and Its Discontents,* p. 86.

27. Freud, *Totem and Taboo,* trans. A. A. Brill (New York: Random House, 1946), p. 202.

28. Freud, *Ego and the Id,* p. 219.

29. Freud, "Instincts and Their Vicissitudes" (1915), trans. Cecil M. Baines, in *Collected Papers,* IV, 70.

30. Freud, "'Civilized' Sexual Morality," p. 87.

31. Freud, *Civilization and Its Discontents,* p. 43.

32. Freud, *Totem and Taboo,* p. 119.

4. Marriage: *Visions of the Daughters of Albion*

1. Freud, "The Taboo of Virginity" (1918), trans. Joan Riviere, in *Collected Papers of Sigmund Freud,* ed. Ernest Jones, 5 vols. (New York: Basic Books, 1959), IV, 217.

2. Freud, "On Narcissism," in *Collected Papers,* IV, 42.

3. Freud, "'Civilized' Sexual Morality and Modern Nervousness" (1908), trans. E. B. Herford and E. Colburn Mayne, in *Collected Papers,* II, 96–97.

4. Freud, "'Civilized' Sexual Morality," pp. 90, 96.

5. Freud, "'Civilized' Sexual Morality," pp. 93, 90.

6. Freud, "'Civilized' Sexual Morality," p. 93.

7. Freud, "'Civilized' Sexual Morality," pp. 98, 90.

8. Freud, "'Civilized' Sexual Morality," p. 97.

9. Freud, "The Most Prevalent Form of Degradation in Erotic Life" (1912), trans. Joan Riviere, from "Contributions to the Psychology of Love," in *Collected Papers,* IV, 211–12.

10. Freud, "Some Psychological Consequences of the Anatomical Distinction Between the Sexes" (1925), trans. James Strachey, in *Collected Papers,* V, 192.

11. Freud, "'Civilized' Sexual Morality," p. 95.

12. Freud, "'Civilized' Sexual Morality," p. 95.

13. Freud, "'Civilized' Sexual Morality," p. 96.

14. Freud, "'Civilized' Sexual Morality," p. 84; italics Freud's.

15. Freud, "The Sexual Aberrations," in *Three Essays on the Theory of Sexuality,* trans. and ed. James Strachey (New York: Basic Books, 1962), p. 31.

16. Freud, "'Civilized' Sexual Morality," p. 84.

17. Freud, "My Views on the Part Played by Sexuality in the Aetiology of the Neuroses" (1905), trans. J. Bernays, in *Collected Papers,* I, 280.

18. Freud, "Female Sexuality," trans. Joan Riviere, in *Collected Papers*, V, 252.

19. Freud, "'Civilized' Sexual Morality," p. 96.

20. Freud, "Sexual Aberrations," p. 26.

21. See my discussion of Freud's terminology in regard to feminine psychology, Chapter 7.

22. Freud, "The Predisposition to Obsessional Neurosis" (1913), trans. Edward Glover and E. Colburn Mayne, in *Collected Papers*, II, 129.

23. Freud, "Infantile Sexuality," in *Three Essays*, p. 50n.

24. Freud, "'Civilized' Sexual Morality," p. 91.

25. Freud, "'Civilized' Sexual Morality," p. 84.

26. Freud, *The Ego and the Id*, in *A General Selection from the Works of Sigmund Freud*, ed. John Rickman, trans. Joan Riviere (Garden City, N.Y.: Doubleday Anchor Books, 1957), p. 227.

27. Freud, "Most Prevalent Form of Degradation," p. 216.

28. Freud, "Most Prevalent Form of Degradation," p. 216.

29. Blake, "A Vision of the Last Judgment."

5. Psychic Organization and Sexual Dialectic in Blake's *Milton*

1. The limitations of reading the prophecies from any one point of view are those of reductionist polemics, which are always potential in extraliterary readings of rich poetic texts; especially so in Blake's case, since his system of thought is radically integrative. The texture of Blake's myth is intricately woven: his theology is political, his politics philosphical, his philosophy a theory of art, his theory of art psychological.

2. It is tempting, for instance, to subject *The Four Zoas* to explication as a psychoanalytic casebook. The result might be profound, or merely slick. My own attempts to discuss *The Four Zoas* as psychoanalytic text in comprehensive terms have thus far been more slick than profound. But I still think that *The Four Zoas* is probably the single richest and most resilient text for reading Blake as psychoanalytic theorist. My relative silence on *The Four Zoas* is the single most compelling reason that I designate this study as introductory.

3. I follow David Erdman's interpretation of Plate 2 in his *The Illuminated Blake* (New York: Anchor Books, 1974), p. 218.

4. Harold Bloom, "Commentary," in *The Poetry and Prose of William Blake*, ed. David V. Erdman (Garden City, N.Y.: Doubleday, 1970), p. 823.

5. Northrop Frye, *Fearful Symmetry* (Princeton: Princeton University Press, 1947). My entire approach to Blake is fundamentally informed

by Frye's seminal study, which remains, in my opinion, the best single reading of Blake. For my disagreements with Frye, see Chapter 6. For Frye's discussion of Blake's system of analogues, see *Fearful Symmetry*, pp. 382–403.

6. Blake does engage in conventional disavowal of his abilities in *Milton* 20:15–19, where he employs the evangelical diction of Psalms, Job, and Ecclesiastes at the culmination of Milton's struggle with Urizen. Here Blake genuinely, and also ironically, personifies the momentary failure of nerve characteristic of the mortal man, who is always "worm" when he perceives himself only as a "cold hand of clay." His "vanity" ironically echoes Koheleth in Ecclesiastes, who always sees himself as small, fated, and helpless, and his God as distant, unfathomable, and all-powerful. But the poet is only momentarily and rhetorically unnerved, for he, as well as Milton, is struggling with the Urizenic and Satanic aspect of himself.

7. I am indebted to Diane Christian for this perception.

8. *The Oxford English Dictionary*, compact ed. (New York: Oxford University Press, 1971), I, 847.

9. Freud, "A Special Type of Object Choice Made by Men" (1910), trans. Joan Riviere, from "Contributions to the Psychology of Love," in *Collected Papers of Sigmund Freud*, ed. Ernest Jones, 5 vols. (New York: Basic Books, 1959), IV, 198.

10. Freud, *Civilization and Its Discontents*, trans. and ed. James Strachey (New York: Norton, 1962), p. 14.

11. Freud, *Totem and Taboo*, trans. A. A. Brill (New York: Random House, 1946), p. 119.

12. Freud, *Civilization and Its Discontents*, p. 15.

13. Freud, "Analysis Terminable and Interminable," trans. Joan Riviere, in *Collected Papers of Sigmund Freud*, ed. Ernest Jones, 5 vols. (New York: Basic Books, 1959), V, 354.

14. Freud, *The Ego and the Id*, in *A General Selection from the Works of Sigmund Freud*, ed. John Rickman, trans. Joan Riviere (Garden City, N.Y.: Doubleday Anchor Books, 1957), p. 222.

15. For reproductions of both sets of Blake's illustrations for *Paradise Lost*, see C. H. Collins Baker, *Catalogue of William Blake's Drawings and Paintings in The Huntington Library*, 2d ed. (San Marino, Calif.: Huntington Library, 1969); and Peter A. Wick and Helen D. Willard, *Water-Color Drawings of William Blake in the Museum of Fine Arts* (Boston: Museum of Fine Arts, 1957). The earlier set (1807) is housed in The Huntington Library, but the Huntington collection also includes the 1808 version of "Satan Comes to the Gates of Hell," which is part of the set at the Boston Fine Arts. For a discussion of the dating of the two sets, see Baker, *Catalogue*, p. 17.

16. Marcia Pointon, *Milton and English Art* (Manchester: Manchester

Notes   243

University Press, 1970), p. 35. According to Pointon, Blake was the only illustrator of Milton successfully to maintain the delicate balance between faithful illustration and unique interpretation.

17. Northrop Frye, "Notes for a Commentary on *Milton*," in *The Divine Vision: Studies in the Poetry and Art of William Blake*, ed. Vivian de Sola Pinto (London, 1957), p. 136.

6. Is She Also the Divine Image? Values for the Feminine in Blake

1. David V. Erdman, *The Illuminated Blake* (Garden City, N.Y.: Doubleday Anchor Books, 1974), p. 272.

2. See Harold Bloom's commentary in *The Poetry and Prose of William Blake*, ed. David V. Erdman (New York: Doubleday, 1970), p. 730. Also see David Bindman, *Blake as an Artist* (Oxford: Phaidon Press, 1977), p. 172.

3. Northrop Frye, "Notes for a Commentary on *Milton*," in *The Divine Vision: Studies in the Poetry and Art of William Blake*, ed. Vivian de Sola Pinto (London, 1957), p. 105. Despite its difficulties or shortcomings, Frye's "Notes" remains an excellent reading of the structure of *Milton*.

4. Frye, "Notes," p. 107.

5. Frye, "Notes," pp. 108-9, 128.

6. Frye, *Fearful Symmetry* (Princeton: Princeton University Press, 1947), p. 75.

7. The remark is written on the back of design number 7, "Hell Canto 4," of Blake's series of illustrations for Dante. The original is now in the Fogg Museum, Cambridge, Massachusetts.

8. Reproduced and discussed in A. S. Roe, *Blake's Illustrations to "The Divine Comedy"* (Princeton: Princeton University Press, 1953), pp. 70-71. Roe's is still the definitive study of the Dante series. Blake's obsession with Female Will in the Dante series leads Roe to mention almost casually that the "natural aspects of this life, as always with Blake, are personified as feminine, while the figures representative of mental and artistic pursuits are masculine. . . . All this is in accord with Blake's basic theories concerning masculine and feminine principles" (p. 190). In fact, of course, Blake's "basic theories" are far broader and deeper than that, as I have tried to indicate. But Roe's reductive formulation is understandable, and in fact indicates the intensity of Blake's ambivalence toward the feminine in his last years. Roe generalizes mistakenly to the whole canon, but if his generalization is restricted to the Dante series, I have no reason to think he is wrong.

9. Susan Fox, "The Female as Metaphor in William Blake's Poetry," *Critical Inquiry* 3, no. 3 (Spring 1977), 513.

10. Blake met Wollstonecraft at the famous weekly dinners hosted by his (and her) employer, Joseph Johnson, publisher of Wordsworth's *Descriptive Sketches*. The depth of Blake's relationship with Wollstonecraft is not known, but critics have suggested that Blake's poem "Mary" may have been about Wollstonecraft. Johnson published her *Original Sketches from Real Life* in 1791, with six illustrations by Blake. Later in the same year, Johnson published Wollstonecraft's *Vindication of the Rights of Woman*. Blake must have been familiar with Wollstonecraft's ideas, even though *Original Sketches from Real Life* are not connected with her feminist theories. There is, however, no extant reference by Blake to Wollstonecraft's feminism. See Mona Wilson, *The Life of William Blake* (London: Oxford University Press, 1971), pp. 44–46.

11. Juliet Mitchell, *Psychoanalysis and Feminism* (New York: Pantheon Books, 1974), p. 5. "There is a formal obeisance to Freud's theories, yet behind most criticism of details there lies an unacknowledged refusal of every major concept."

12. An overview of Blake criticism on the subject of women and feminine principles is in order. With a few exceptions, major Blake critics of the twentieth century have addressed themselves to Blake's values for the feminine indirectly, by discussing the system of contraries, the role of the emanation, and the Female Will. Northrop Frye's analysis in *Fearful Symmetry* and "Notes for a Commentary on *Milton*" is among the most penetrating, as I have noted, but his diction suggests that in eternity, Blake's female is absorbed into the male, rather than male and female into a humanity. "The worship of a female principle, . . . specifically a maternal principle, is not imaginative and is only possible to natural religion. In Eden there is no Mother-God. . . . In the more highly developed (religions) God is always the Supreme Male, the creator for whom the distinction between the beloved female and the created child has disappeared" (*Symmetry*, p. 75). If Frye does not quite do justice to Blake on this point, it may be because a final synthesis of the sexes in a genderless humanity remains ambiguously expressed in Blake's works.

David Erdman's *Prophet against Empire* (Garden City, N.Y.: Doubleday Anchor Books, 1969) relegates the problem of Blake's thought on this issue to footnote references, though he clearly realizes it is a problem: ". . . the males must continue to stand for both mankind and womankind—a difficulty of many man-made allegories—so that Blake's hostility to 'female will,' for example, is not easy to evaluate" (253). Following Erdman's footnotes to an earlier phase of modern Blake criticism, I have found a tendency toward simplistic pronouncements. D. S.

Sloss and J. P. R. Wallis discussed Blake's view of women extensively and reductively, concluding that "he was no feminist. He persuaded himself that he had highest spiritual sanction for asserting the supremacy of the masculine genius" (*The Prophetic Writings of William Blake* [Oxford: Clarendon Press, 1926], II, 441). Sloss and Wallis see a direct correlation between Female Will and woman, but apparently none between Jerusalem and woman.

Harold Bloom sidesteps the issue, but he does not preclude the possibility that woman in Blake's eternity may be subject rather than object: "Jerusalem may best be understood as . . . the freedom of the redeemed man from every institutionalized restraint on his spiritual freedom . . . the beloved creation or potential creation of the fully imaginative man . . . both city and woman, where one lives and what one loves, when both are as they ought to be" ("Commentary," in *Poetry and Prose*, p. 849). Bloom's choice of terms, like Frye's and often like Blake's, makes it somewhat difficult for a woman to identify with that comprehensive "fully imaginative man." Foster Damon's *A Blake Dictionary* (Providence: Brown University Press, 1965) devotes the expected attention to Female Will, under that heading and many others. Damon sees Jerusalem in female terms only incidentally, and specifies that "the domination of woman, Blake believed, is one of the greatest forces corrupting society" (447). His mention of the androgyne is instructive, if confusing. "The opposite of the Hermaphrodite is the Androgyne, in which man's bisexual nature is perfectly harmonized. This was his original state" (182). I might add that although Blake used the term "hermaphrodite" frequently and always pejoratively, he did not ever use the word "androgyne."

Bernard Blackstone's *English Blake* (Hamden, Conn.: Archon Books, 1966) is tonally remarkable for its discussion of Blake and the feminine. "Blake, like many other poets, noticed that it is the cheap and flashy qualities in a man which most impress women; they despise intelligence, gentleness, and any unusual power. Again, perhaps, they are fundamentally afraid that intelligence in the man may rob them of their dominion and so they feel it safer to stick to the stupid" (294). Speaking for himself and for Blake, Blackstone calls deceit "a woman's chief quality." Woman is consoled for her loss of delight in life by "the mysteries of religion, by the pomp and ceremonies which act so efficiently on her weaker intelligence. But man has no such compensation, if he is virile and impatient of humbug" (296). Blackstone, one imagines, considers himself very virile. He is a fine example of the critic whose reading of literature is distorted by his own disappointments and biases. But Blackstone is not dismissible because he is so plainly misogynistic. His reading is based on close explication, and nothing he says is really inaccurate from the vantage point of one perspective in the Blakean universe. He, or any defender of such a reading, could quote chapter and verse to support that reading. The tone, of course, is quite another matter, having little to do with Blake and everything to do with Blackstone.

Denis Saurat's *Blake and Milton* (New York: Russell & Russell, 1965) decides that although the woman is valuable to Blake, a "power concerned in the very making and vivifying of the universe," still "man is predominant; woman being only the softer, weaker side of him. . . . For Blake, as for Milton, the leadership of Woman is the source of all evil" (115). Of the essential differences between the two poets on this topic, and of Blake's specific disagreement with Milton, there is no detailed discussion.

There are many other major critics to whom I might give a paragraph or two, but I believe the major positions and perspectives are well represented by those I have discussed. Instead of reiterating established views through other standard critical voices, I shall conclude with comments on a psychological study and a feminist study. June Singer's *The Unholy Bible: A Psychological Interpretation of William Blake* (New York: Harper & Row, Colophon Books, 1970) gives more comprehensive attention to sexual dialectic in Blake than do most other sources, and much of Singer's discussion is excellent. (My qualifications and disagreements with her will be plain to the reader.) When anima is suppressed, "man's sensitivity to the feminine acquires a particularly numinous quality; that is, his repressed femininity acquires an inexplicable power over his male side, leading him into an exercise of his irrational functions" (26); "Man must acknowledge and come to terms with the feminine principle within himself, he must know her in her nakedness for what she is—an integral part of his own psyche" (90). In her extensive discussion of the Proverbs of Hell, Singer chooses "Let man wear the fell of the lion, woman the fleece of the sheep" as the focal point for Blake's ideas about "natural psychological differences between the sexes" (88). She summarizes Blake's ideal of the creative sexual relationship in "The cistern contains; the fountain overflows." The vessel that gives form to life is the woman; the ever moving, dynamic force is the male. Singer is concerned to find only correspondences between Blake and Jung, not oppositions or contraries. The result is that Blake inevitably comes out looking like Jung. Nevertheless, Singer's study is worth a careful reading for its numerous fine passages.

My text disagrees with Susan Fox's fine article "The Female as Metaphor in William Blake's Poetry," which appeared in the Spring 1977 issue of *Critical Inquiry*. That disagreement, which I expand to make a point, may tend to obscure my basic and more profound agreements with Fox's work. "In his prophetic poems Blake perceives a perfection of humanity defined in part by the complete mutuality of its interdependent genders." But contrary to his own ideal, Blake "represents one of those mutual, contrary, equal genders as inferior and dependent . . . or as unnaturally and disastrously dominant" (507). Although Fox is sympathetic to Blake's historical situation, she is not content to explain him out of his self-imposed contradictions by calling them metaphoric, because to do so is "to beg the question of what a metaphor is anyway and why one chooses it" (509). Her conclusion is that "metaphors are not divorced from concepts. When they conflict with the concepts they are meant to advance they attest to an uneasiness in their author's mind" (519). For a discussion of this subject which successfully justifies Blake's position, see Irene Taylor's excellent essay "The Woman Scaly," *Midwestern Modern Language Association Bulletin* 6, no. 1 (Spring 1973), 74–87.

13. Mitchell, *Psychoanalysis and Feminism,* pp. 137ff.

14. The Tate Gallery's 1978 Blake exhibition was reviewed in such publications as *Time* magazine. I regard that recognition as an indication that Blake's visibility on the popular market, as differentiated from the scholarly market, is still increasing.

15. For a discussion of Freud's theories on feminine psychology, see Chapter 7.

7. Freud and Feminine Psychology

1. Freud, "The Psychogenesis of a Case of Homosexuality in a Woman" (1920), trans. Barbara Low and R. Gabler, in *Collected Papers of Sigmund Freud,* ed. Ernest Jones, 5 vols. (New York: Basic Books, 1959), II, 231.

2. Freud, "Analysis Terminable and Interminable" (1937), trans. Joan Riviere, in *Collected Papers,* V, 355.

3. Freud, "The Infantile Genital Organization of the Libido" (1923), trans. Joan Riviere, in *Collected Papers,* II, 249.

4. Freud, "Transformations of Puberty," in *Three Essays on the Theory of Sexuality,* trans. and ed. James Strachey (New York: Basic Books, 1962), p. 85n.

5. Freud, "Transformations of Puberty," p. 86n.

6. Freud, "'A Child Is Being Beaten': A Contribution to the Study of the Origin of Sexual Perversions," trans. Alix and James Strachey, in *Collected Papers,* II, 199.

7. Freud, *Civilization and Its Discontents,* trans. and ed. James Strachey (New York: Norton, 1962), p. 53n.

8. Freud, "The Sexual Aberrations," in *Three Essays*, p. 26.

9. Freud, "The Predisposition to Obsessional Neurosis" (1913), trans. Edward Glover and E. Colburn Mayne, in *Collected Papers*, II, 128.

10. Freud, "Some Psychological Consequences of the Anatomical Distinction between the Sexes" (1925), trans. James Strachey, in *Collected Papers*, V, 194.

11. Freud, "Female Sexuality," trans. Joan Riviere, in *Collected Papers*, V, 255.

12. Freud, "Analysis Terminable and Interminable," p. 354.

13. Freud, "Psychogenesis of a Case of Homosexuality," p. 211.

14. Freud, "The Sexual Aberrations," in *Three Essays*, p. 17.

15. Freud, "On Narcissism," trans. Cecil M. Baines, in *Collected Papers*, IV, 44-45.

16. Freud, "The Passing of the Oedipus Complex" (1924), trans. Joan Riviere, in *Collected Papers*, II, 275.

17. Freud, "Female Sexuality," p. 263.

18. Freud, "Passing of the Oedipus Complex," p. 274.

19. Freud, "The Taboo of Virginity," trans. Joan Riviere, in *Collected Papers*, IV, 223-24.

20. Freud, "Analysis Terminable and Interminable," pp. 349, 350.

21. Freud, "Analysis Terminable and Interminable," p. 354.

22. Freud, "Analysis Terminable and Interminable," pp. 356, 357.

23. Freud, "Analysis Terminable and Interminable," p. 354.

Afterwords: New Jerusalem and Old Rome

1. Freud, *Civilization and Its Discontents*, trans. and ed. James Strachey (New York: Norton, 1962), p. 17.

2. Freud, *Civilization and Its Discontents*, p. 17.

3. Freud, *Civilization and Its Discontents*, p. 18.

Index

BLAKE *and* FREUD

Designed by Richard E. Rosenbaum.
Composed by The Composing Room of Michigan, Inc.
in 10 point Baskerville V.I.P., 3 points leaded,
with display lines in Baskerville.
Printed offset by Thomson/Shore, Inc. on
Warren's Number 66 Antique Offset, 50 pound basis.
Bound by John H. Dekker & Sons, Inc.
in Holliston book cloth
and stamped in All Purpose foil.

Library of Congress Cataloging in Publication Data

George, Diana Hume, 1948–
  Blake and Freud.

  Includes bibliographical references and index.
    1. Blake, William, 1757–1827—Knowledge—Psychology.   2. Freud, Sig-
  mund, 1856–1939.   3. Psychoanalysis and literature.   I. Title.
PR4148.P8G4   821'.7   80-11244
ISBN 0-8014-1286-2